MICRO
MESSAGING

MICRO MESSAGING

Why Great Leadership Is Beyond Words

STEPHEN YOUNG

New York   Chicago   San Francisco   Athens
London   Madrid   Mexico City   Milan
New Delhi   Singapore   Sydney   Toronto

2 3 4 5 6 7 8 9   QFR   21 20 19 18

ISBN   978-1-259-86096-6
MHID   1-259-86096-5

McGraw-Hill Education books are available at special quantity discounts to use as premiums and sales promotions or for use in corporate training programs. To contact a representative, please visit the Contact Us pages at www.mhprofessional.com.

Library of Congress Cataloging-in-Publication Data
Names: Young, Stephen, author.
Title: Micromessaging : why great leadership is beyond words / by Stephen Young.
Other titles: Micro messaging
Description: 2 Edition. | New York : McGraw-Hill Education, 2016. | Revised edition of the author's MicroMessaging, c2007.
Identifiers: LCCN 2016037554| ISBN 9781259860966 (paperback) | ISBN 1259860965
Subjects: LCSH: Communication in management—Psychological aspects. | Body language. | Executives—Attitudes. | Leadership—Psychological aspects. | Employee motivation. | BISAC: BUSINESS & ECONOMICS / Leadership.
Classification: LCC HD30.3 .Y68 2016 | DDC 658.4/5—dc23 LC record available at https://lccn.loc.gov/2016037554

Dedicated to Alex and Austin

Thank you for demonstrating that wisdom

is not dependent on age.

Acknowledgments

The creation of this book and my consulting firm Insight Education Systems are due to the dedication, vision, and collaboration of Barbara Hockfield. She has been the wizard behind the curtain leading the journey to my Emerald City and home again. There truly are muses.

Mary Rowe, thank you for your scholarly work on the power of subtle communication, for coining the term "micro-inequity," and your ongoing collaboration and personal support.

Heidi Guber, your insight and persistence encouraging the pursuit of this dream has brought it to reality.

Special appreciation to: Deb Dagit, Phylis Piano, Bill Swanson, Ted Childs, Luke Visconti, Sylvia Allen, Lisa Jing, Rohini Anand, JPMorganChase, Rev. Jesse Jackson, William H. Gray, Joyce Tucker, Roz Hudnell, Terri Jessen, Barbara Bessey, Laurie Horenstein, Texanna Reeves, Charles Jackson, Kim Davis, Johnetta Cole, Laura Quintana, Mike Silvaggi, Jennifer Allyn, Elsie Jackson, Gustavo de la Torre, Jim Rector, and Sheila Wellington for their support as champions of this program at its inception.

Many thanks to the following companies who have brought the concepts of this book into their organizations: American Express,

Apple Computer, Applied Materials, Bank of America, BASF, BMW, Boeing, Campbell Soup Company, Cisco Systems, Catalyst, Citibank, The Coca Cola Company, The Conference Board, Daimler Chrysler, Dell Computer, Duke Realty, Federal Reserve Bank, Ford Motor Company, Frito Lay, Genentech, General Motors, Georgia Pacific, Gillette, Guidant, Hearst Publishing, IBM, Intel, Intuit, Kaiser Permanente, Key Bank, Kodak, Lockheed Martin, McDermott Will & Emery LLP, Medco Health, Medtronic, Merck, Motorola, People's Bank, Price Waterhouse, Prudential Insurance, Raytheon, Reuters, Schering Plough, Securities Industry Association, Shearman and Sterling LLP, Shell Oil, Skadden Arps LLP, Sodexho, Standard & Poors, Starbucks, Sunoco, Texas Instruments, Unilever, UPS, Weil Gotshal & Manges LLP, Wells Fargo, W.R. Gore.

Thanks to Lorraine Kreahling for editing the manuscript.

MI, JL, PS, CW, SD, TB—please read this book.

Contents

Preface

Be careful of your thoughts,
they become words.
Be careful of your words,
they become actions.
Be careful of your actions,
they become habits.
Be careful of your habits,
they become character.
Be careful of your character,
it becomes your destiny...

—Unknown

When we write or speak a message, our egocentrism can cause us to believe that what we intend to convey is what others will interpret. Unfortunately, interpretation and intent don't always match up. While there is usually some overlap of common understanding, rarely is the match congruent. That gap between message sent and message received often determines fear, confidence, comfort, loyalty, and the motivation to perform at our peak levels.

The words of language are what we use on the intellectual level to determine the messages others communicate to us. This codified structure of language limits our ability to read the depth and richness of the underlying message. As thinking beings, we give priority to the intellectual codified structure of words. We allow it to dominate what we determine that a message should be conveying. The more subtle and nearly impossible to articulate micromessages take a back seat. Language is after all a major factor that distinguishes us as the higher species. Language is also the principle reason we have dulled our ability to read the subtle messages that reveal far more truth than words.

Someone once compared the elusiveness of micromessages to describing a dream. You know the dream occurred. You know what and how you felt, but it is too amorphous to be described in a way that makes sense to anyone else, or even to yourself for that matter.

Micromessages convey feelings that inform us whether it is safe to express our views that we do or don't fit in and whether we are valued, even when we can't identify the specifics that convey those feelings.

Countless times we have all walked away from a conversation or meeting with someone not knowing exactly why we felt uncomfortable, devalued, or marginalized. You may have mumbled to yourself, *I can't put my finger on it but...*, confident that the feeling wasn't mere paranoia. The person you were speaking with said all the right things, but somehow you departed with coldness, convincingly covered by a facade of politeness. With nothing tangible to articulate, you charge it to being oversensitive.

How could you ever confront someone about something so amorphous and indefinable? The concepts of this book are about just that; learning how to put our finger on it and uncover the underlying messages that reveal people's true feelings. More importantly, you will learn to convert what you feel into codified language for others to understand how their messages may be influencing your behaviors.

When a reporting relationship exists between the sender and receiver of the message, and the messages are left unaddressed, nothing short of a virus is unleashed, infecting the leader's effectiveness as well as the recipient's engagement and performance. Never underestimate the "power of small."

Micromessages, which comprise microinequities and their positive counterpart microadvantages, are the central threads of mammalian communication. The trumpeting of an elephant over great distances and the squeal of a mongoose ringing through the jungle send messages of caution, courtship, danger, or sorrow without the structure of language. The tonal qualities and nuance of the sound is unmistakably clear to all born to interpret the message. Humans, however, in our evolution have language which jams our radar for interpreting micromessages.

Words do make the process of communication easier, but they also make it easy to use prepackaged *word packets* of deception that rarely get challenged. We can use these word packets to communicate what we think others need to hear, even though the packet doesn't remotely represent our genuine feelings or truth.

We simply *select* a packet off the shelf—such as, "That was a great presentation," or "You have such good insight," or "How could we have ever done it without you?"—and then toss it where and when it is needed. The packet contains the right words, so there is nothing to challenge.

As a parent, off-the-shelf word packets allow me to routinely respond to my daughter's frequently asked question safely, "Dad, how does this outfit look on me?"

I select the perfect prepackaged response and deliver it. Occasionally I slip up and get caught speaking the words before actually looking up. No problem—just press reset, wait five seconds, and resend the message.

If I had to respond nonverbally with facial expressions alone, the true message would come ringing through, yielding one of two results. She would either retreat to her bedroom and don a new outfit or would shake her head and announce, "I don't care that you don't like it, I'm wearing it anyway!" The familiar packets allow her to ignore the nonverbal micromessages and default to the precision of the actual words stated.

Managers in the workplace send these packets in abundance. It is a convenient way to avoid uncomfortable confrontations. After all, the employee's work performance isn't really *that* bad, so why stir things up?

We allow words to obscure the interpretation of the deeper meaning.

Though subtle, the micromessages communicate critical information often overlooked. In the world of leadership we find ourselves the victim of something Paul Graves, a colleague, calls the "snapback" effect. Like elastic, our minds expand when we are shown new and innovative concepts. We routinely stretch and embrace new perspectives with an almost limitless capacity. As we stretch, we nod, smile, send signals of understanding, and even commit to take action.

When we step back into our daily routine and there is no external force pushing, behaviors tend to *snap back* to their original position. People tend to be more comfortable when they are not stretched, yet it is at this point that energy is at its greatest.

This book is all about stretching and sustaining a new position of energy.

You will no longer receive a word packet and process it with a preconditioned response. Your interpretation of every message will feel incomplete without its accompanying micromessage that goes beyond the spoken words.

The power of leadership rests in one's fluency in speaking the language of influence and motivation. Micromessages are the heart and soul of leadership.

Asleep in the Fire
The Danger of Unconscious Bias Training

U nconscious bias is the premise upon which the messages in this book are rooted. But is a focus on unconscious bias the silver bullet that so many seem to suggest, or does it merely have us shooting blanks on our quest for a truly inclusive workplace?

The critical paradox is that unconscious bias is an *intangible* state of mind—a cerebral concept and, therefore, not actionable. One cannot "do" an unconscious bias. As long as we remain focused on the *concept* side of the equation we cannot effect change. It is entirely the *action* side of the equation that generates results.

This book reveals the solution and the tools to bridge the gap between the conceptual state of mind and the truly actionable solutions that drive change.

Raising our awareness through unconscious bias training can fool us into thinking we've made great progress in managing it. But there is a risk. Many people walk away from these experiences feeling better informed. They become comfortable having learned the root cause of the problems they perpetuate or experience. But these "aha" moments are simply not good enough.

There is a dangerous self-deception in thinking this knowledge makes us an active part of the solution.

Simply being informed and made aware does not make us equipped to influence change. No more than knowing about and talking about global warming will result in fewer icebergs melting this week.

When we look at the definition of unconscious bias a notable paradox emerges.

Unconscious Bias: *The opinions we hold about others that are influenced through past experiences, forming filters that cause conclusions to be reached about groups or ethnicities, by means other than active thought or reasoning.*

The paradox is revealed in three key words: "opinions," "filters," and "conclusions"—after all, no one can "do" an opinion, filter, or a conclusion. These are entirely limited to cerebral thoughts and feelings. When we act on those thoughts and feelings and convert them into action, they become microinequities.

The only way for organizations to effectively manage unconscious bias is by learning how to manage the subtle micromessages we send that reveal them—typically, microinequities.

These micromessages, whether they come in the form of destructive microinequities or developmental microadvantages, function as the core of how unconscious bias is manifested and how workplace inclusion is ultimately achieved.

Many organizations tend to focus primarily on educating their staff on the eye-opening world of unconscious bias. This often leaves attendees knowledgeable, but without the skill to effect change.

There are countless examples of people who leave unconscious bias training experiences with a blissful "aha" cloud of newfound awareness.

They emerge enlightened and enthusiastic, but ill-equipped to personally drive change. Why is this?

There is great danger in focusing on unconscious bias instead of directing our attention to the micromessages. It is *entirely* through the micromessages, which are the manifestations of unconscious bias, that we become able to address and fix the effects of unconscious bias.

Our lack of awareness of how to manage our micromessages often leaves us asleep in the fire.

There are countless data points, articles, and training programs that uncover a long history of unconscious bias in the workplace. These spend a disproportionate focus on causes and impact of unconscious bias. They report our failures and serve up an abundance of data for the disparate treatment certain groups receive, based on factors and behaviors of which we have been unaware.

The focus tends to be more about the "what" or condition of the problem instead of identifying the specific process by which we can take action, as individuals, to correct it.

For example, learning that 60 percent of American CEOs are over six feet tall, yet less than 15 percent of American men are over that height is an interesting and revealing statistic—but what do we DO about it?

Data revealing that overweight people are given lower performance appraisal ratings provides another "aha" moment and may be enlightening, but again, offers no actionable solution.

Discovering that candidates with ethnic sounding names receive a lower percentage of callbacks for an interview is eye opening information that heightens awareness but the question remains, what specifically am I expected to do about that *tomorrow morning*?

Let's face it, no one is expected to interview all short people, or give higher performance ratings to those who are overweight. Spending time learning about these, and countless other ways, that our unconscious biases are manifested is introspective, analytical, and even interesting.

Often, a great amount of training time and resources are allocated to build an awareness of unconscious bias. Participants are thrilled at having achieved newfound knowledge of the impact of unconscious bias, yet are left puzzled about what day-to-day actions to take to remediate the condition.

The traditional training approach places the focus on those unfortunate "others" who are affected by unconscious bias. However, putting special focus on specific groups, based on their differences, is ineffective.

It identifies the broader problem while offering no actionable solution. It makes it very difficult for any individual to return to the workplace and take meaningful action, ultimately causing many to view the experience as yet another "warm and fuzzy, touchy feely" expenditure of time.

In short order, people find themselves frustrated and wondering how to implement change. What exactly am I expected to do with my newfound awareness?

In a survey conducted of mid-level managers for a New Jersey–based pharmaceutical company, a series of questions were asked about their participation in unconscious bias training.

The results were eye-opening. Two of the survey questions were:

1. Do you feel you have a clear understanding of unconscious bias?
2. Do you understand what you can do to remedy the condition?

In response to the first question, 73 percent of survey respondents indicated they had a clear understanding of unconscious bias. Remarkably, 92 percent of the respondents could not identify, specifically, what they could do to address it.

In this case, the "bullet" designed to target unconscious bias became a blank.

The underlying causes for our behavior are not as important as identifying the benefits we derive from taking specific actions that enable us to be more effective leaders and colleagues.

To truly move the needle forward, the workplace must focus on managing the controllable elements that alter the impact of our unconscious biases—the micromessages, microinequities, and microadvantages we send.

Since this book's original publishing, the MicroInequities seminar has been taken to 35 countries in every region, worldwide. The concept resonates globally because it gets to the "DNA" of how all humans communicate, particularly in the ways we inspire, motivate, and enable others to perform.

This book provides the specific actions and tools needed to actively manage unconscious bias in the workplace.

CHAPTER 1

Setting the Stage

It was Monday morning, which meant yet another routine staff meeting. Our manager pulled the eight of us on her team together as many as four times a week for updates on virtually imperceptible changes in our projects. The meetings were unscripted but so predictable that everyone practically mouthed all the words. The afternoons were filled with one-on-one discussions with our manager, in which we used a variety of creative synonyms to describe what had already been reported to the group. Extensive filler was generally required here.

No one ever complained about the constant meetings. So, I did what most of us might do: I interpreted the silence as compliance. But there was another silence quietly building.

My manager and I just didn't get along, though I'm sure neither of us could articulate precisely why. I kept all my feelings about her incompetence under wraps, so it had to be something other than that. I just chalked it up to the proverbial bad chemistry. After all, when you can't put your finger on something, what else could it be? But it was clear we didn't click.

In the meetings, when it was my turn to talk, I always noticed a special expression she seemed to reserve just for me. A blank look of indifference, a look-through-me stare, droopy slow eye blinks. My comments received no nod of understanding like those given colleagues. And while I spoke, she seemed to become very concerned about what time of day it was. She certainly wasn't paying much attention to my report, so what could she be pondering, I wondered? Her lunch date? I had no idea.

Her lack of attention to my report and her general insensitivity were irritating, but I couldn't tell if anyone else noticed. Was she purposely ignoring my work, or was there something else going on? I wasn't sure.

Then after one of our meetings, in which I had completed another project review with the same feelings I always had around her, another team member, who occasionally fell victim to the manager's scorn, leaned over and whispered, "Will these microinequities ever stop?" Wow! I had never heard that term before, but it fit my experience perfectly. Microinequities.

The manager's actions were all so subtle that they could never be fully described with words. Any attempt to bring attention to her aberrant eye movement, changes in breathing pattern, resistant hand gestures, or anything that wouldn't pass hard and tangible courtroom evidence standards would leave me sounding hypersensitive or overreactive. Still, those small slights left me feeling as though I was not as worthy as others. At least now I had a name for them. They were *microinequities*.

I didn't know it that day but I was onto something that would become anything but "micro" in my own life and the lives of hundreds of thousands of corporate executives, office workers, students, teachers, relatives, and couples with whom I have shared these insights. What I eventually learned about the ways we send and receive these minute, nearly invisible, nuanced messages would extend well beyond the effects of conventional discrimi-

> *With an awareness of microinequities comes the opportunity for leaders at all levels to eliminate such behavior and to improve the performance and morale of those they work with.*

nation. These micromessages are the true epicenter, defining a leader's ability to influence others for better or worse.

With an awareness of microinequities comes the opportunity for leaders at all levels to eliminate such behavior and to improve the performance and morale of those they work with. The flip side of the damage that microinequities inflict is the potential that positive micromessages hold for improving working relationships and organizational performance.

Effective use of micromessages by leaders lies at the core of what inspires followers to follow. If that sounds grandiose, prepare to be converted. By the time you finish this book, you'll be a staunch advocate of the concept. Whether one of the many Fortune 500 CEOs or an entry-level professional, everyone has been on the receiving end of a micromessage. But imagine the potential results from harnessing the subtle power of such behavior. Becoming aware of micromessaging can deliver visible and measurable results without compromising your personal business style.

> *Effective use of micromessages by leaders lies at the core of what inspires followers to follow.*

Unaddressed, negative micromessages accumulate, wear down, and infect an otherwise healthy self-esteem. Just because negative micromessages aren't obvious doesn't mean they aren't damaging to the individual *and* the organization. In fact, pretending negative micromessages don't occur can be dangerous.

My five-year-old nephew drove this point home to me recently. He dropped his cookie on the floor of the Amtrak station men's room, then picked it up and wiped off the visible grunge in preparation to eat it. When I took it away, explaining it was too dirty and might make him sick, he replied, "I wiped it off. Don't you know if you can't see the dirt, it's not there?"

"If you can't see it, it's not there." This is the silent mantra by which too many business professionals operate. If you can't see

Pretending negative micromessages don't occur can be dangerous.

something clearly, and aren't able to articulate it, it's okay to proceed as if it's not there. Many professionals convince themselves that trying to describe an inequity, to raise awareness, may only make matters worse. This delusional behavior is why microinequities continue.

This book will explore what really goes on when hand gestures, facial expressions, or the tone of voice don't match the words being spoken. In fact, they frequently don't match. We will pull back the curtain on what causes us to decide how we are going to respond long before someone is finished speaking. Why and what does it mean when we scrutinize one person's work for the flaws while accepting the brilliance of another's without a second thought? Some people just can't have a good idea, because of who they are, while others offer unintelligible recommendations we're willing to

This book will explore what really goes on when hand gestures, facial expressions, or the tone of voice don't match the words being spoken.

assume have merit. These are the micromessages that cause leaders either to shut down or to unlock the potential of those they influence.

Developing the skill and language to identify and address negative micromessages puts a new power in your grasp. You will no longer be confused by feeling something, but not be able to put your finger on the negative reaction you sense. Instead, you will be in a position to confront microinequities and reduce the damage they inflict.

You will not fix every conflict or get everything you want with this new skill, but you will be able to identify what either drags us down or enhances our performance. This new skill will enable you to rally everyone around you with micromessages that inspire, motivate, and get beyond conventional rhetoric.

You will read about proven connections between micromessaging and the corporate bottom line. Using micromessaging, leaders have propelled teams to amazing achievements, solidified relationships, opened new doors of creativity and innovation, and transformed organizations.

> *Developing the skill and language to identify and address negative micromessages puts a new power in your grasp.*

Some leaders leverage their power and authority to get people to perform. It's a leadership style that works, but not without limitations: People live up to *your* expectations, not *their* potential. What you instruct them to do is *all* they will do for you. They will do precisely what you direct them to do—nothing more, though sometimes less. Innovation, creativity, commitment, and loyalty don't play into that equation. The *power* approach results in an employee experience that is transactional, the manager directs and the employee complies. It is also transitional, employees quit as soon as they find a way out.

No matter who you are, at some point you have undoubtedly been on the receiving end of the microinequities equation. We've all had a conversation with someone who, though they didn't move an eyelash or a single facial muscle, somehow clearly communicated the message: "The sooner I get away from you, the happier I will be." On the other hand, a wide smile, direct gaze, and hearty handshake don't always convey admiration. Sending the micromessages that convey your intended message requires a deep understanding of how others interpret truth or see through the pretense.

> *This new skill will enable you to rally everyone around you with micromessages that inspire, motivate, and get beyond conventional rhetoric.*

Micromessages can inspire confidence and enable an individual to stretch for higher goals, or they can undermine a worker's self-confidence and cause him or her to second guess every decision. They have the power to do this with barely a spoken word.

Consider the boss who looks up when you walk into his office, makes eye contact, welcomes you, smiles, stands to greet you, builds on your remarks, asks your opinion, and expresses appreciation for the report you have brought him. He frames his micromessages in ways that inspire, motivate, and cause your inhibitions and fears to drift away. Of course, there is also the boss who barely acknowledges your presence, constantly stares at his screen while you speak, seems pained to have to deal with you and your issues, does most of the talking, asks no questions, never moves from his chair, and often points to a blank area on his desk to say, "Just put it there." He uses micromessages to convey disappointment and disapproval, but rarely provides objective feedback explaining his sentiment. He just hopes you'll get it through intuition.

> *Micromessages can inspire confidence and enable an individual to stretch for higher goals, or they can undermine a worker's self-confidence and cause him or her to second guess every decision.*

My search to learn more about microinequities—the subtle messages that devalue and discourage performance—led me to some landmark research by Mary P. Rowe, PhD, at MIT's Sloan School of Management. Dr. Rowe coined the term *microinequity* in her investigation of the underlying cause of why some students felt included while others did not.

According to Dr. Rowe, "Microinequities have a double power punch: First, they exclude the person who is different, making her feel on the outside. Second, exclusion undermines an individual's self-confidence and makes him less productive. So, etiquette aside, microinequities are bad business practice."[1] The more I learned about Dr. Rowe's research, the more I realized she had laid the groundwork for interpreting language in an entirely new way, using a powerful system of translation and communication. I recognized that an understanding of microinequities could accelerate leadership effectiveness.

Micromessaging—communicating with other human beings through visual, audible, sublingual means, no doubt predates our ability to speak. We actually read micromessages quite naturally without thinking about them. You might say human beings read each other's micromessages subconsciously, in the same way that one dog understands another dog is unfriendly simply because the dog's fur is standing on end. The dogs read each other perfectly. It's not all that different for people. When someone treats you with disrespect, you may feel your own hair standing on end.

In my case, it was too risky to confront the manager who was making my hair stand up. There was no common language with which to address the problem. Just imagine my saying, "I notice that every time I offer an idea at our meetings you get a blank look on your face and blink your eyes a little more slowly." Or, "You consistently rest your chin in your palm and breath more deeply than usual when I am speaking." Ironically, if I were ever to approach her with those accusations she would likely roll her eyes, look blank, rest her chin in her palm, take a few deep breaths, and sigh before escorting me to the door.

Unfortunately, without a new common language, and the ability to communicate what was happening in a way that made sense to her, my observations would have fallen on deaf ears. And even more unfortunately, she didn't recognize the impact her responses were having on my performance: I increasingly withdrew from con-

---

[1] Mary P. Rowe, "Barriers to Equality: The Power of Subtle Discrimination to Maintain Unequal Opportunity." *Employee Responsibilities and Rights Journal,* Vol. 3, No. 2, 1990. pp. 153–163.

tributing, rarely risked offering ideas beyond the conventional, and felt my loyalty and motivation flagging. If my reaction was typical, imagine what is happening to other workers in other organizations across the globe. Astonishingly, only slight shifts in these micromessages can motivate those you rely on to deliver at unexpected levels of performance.

Employees who receive negative micromessages come to work feeling undervalued and tend to focus on merely getting the assigned work done. A case in point is a second-year associate at a law firm I interviewed, who said that before she was exposed to the concept of micromessaging, she used to "Look in the mirror and see myself as a living and breathing 3CPO." She was a robot with a pulse. Everything she did was a mechanized transactional process in which she had no emotional investment, because of how the managing partner communicated with her.

However, there were others to whom the managing partner expressed a very different set of messages. For example, there was one associate who was blindly respected even when he presented bad ideas. He was encouraged to be a free thinker, to offer the wildest innovative concepts. Only half the time did those off-the-wall ideas ever work, but the half that succeeded ultimately led him to bigger opportunities. Such variations in communication reveal the blind spot of leadership. They are at the heart of why some careers thrive and others wither. And they explain why some leaders truly inspire top performance, while others merely mouth the words.

> The most damaging outcome of microinequities is that we never really know an individual's unfettered potential.

Dr. Rowe puts it this way, "the mechanisms of prejudice against persons of difference, however, usually small in nature, but not trivial in effect, are especially powerful and damaging taken together." Most people initially associate the damage done by microinequities with minorities and women. Although it is true that some groups receive a disproportionate volume of microinequities in the workplace, the fact is, every group gets them and all aspects of work are affected. Being on the wrong side of the merger, style of dress, age, physical size, which people you choose to befriend, and even your attractiveness are common causes for receiving microinequities. The most damaging outcome of microinequities is that we never really know an individual's unfettered potential.

Microadvantages, positive micromessaging, do quite the opposite. Microadvantages act as catalysts that unleash potential and results. They encourage the out-of-the-box thinking everyone rhetorically says is so vital. A number of Fortune 500 companies have measured the impact work in positive micromessaging has had on their leadership process. The effect has been a sort of trickle down, up, around, and out result. Managers use

> *Microadvantages act as catalysts that unleash potential and results.*

the process to drive the performance of their direct reports, employees at all levels use the skills upward to repair or improve relations with their managers, colleagues apply it to all aspects of peer relationships, and nearly everyone takes it home to address the multitude of issues with family and friends.

The following exceptional results were reported at Merck :

In a longitudinal study Merck conducted six to nine months after our employees attended the Microinequities seminar, 90 percent of employees said they were aware of the micromessages they send and receive. Fifty-five percent indicated that they had had conversations with others at work regarding a micromessage resulting in improved: work team norms, communication skills, and meeting norms. This resulted in an 85 percent reported improvement in business relationships. Not only do our employees really enjoy the highly engaging

Microinequities program, they apply what they learn leading to a more inclusive work environment and better business outcomes as we unleash the full potential of our talent.

Deborah Dagit, Merck[2]

As businesses become more diverse and global, and the marketplace more competitive, a different set of strategies is needed to aggressively manage corporate culture. Multinational corporations have begun using the micromessaging concepts to bridge the gap between international cultural differences, with companies in fourteen countries having already adopted the practice of micromessaging as of this book's release date. Broadening the application of this knowledge and skill across borders shaves away much of the cultural divide between continents and countries.

> *The discovery of a means to decode micromessages is like the discovery of a new sort of multidimensional mirror—one that will allow you to see the often invisible dimensions of your own behavior, comprehend what others see, and recognize how you can adjust the lens through which they view you.*

The discovery of a means to decode micromessages is like the discovery of a new sort of multidimensional mirror—one that will allow you to see the often invisible dimensions of your own behavior, comprehend what others see, and recognize how you can adjust the lens through which they view you. What you do with what you see is up to you. In addition to helping you discover what you *look like* in this new mirror—this book will also offer techniques, tools, and key lessons to build and sustain your knowledge and skill in positive micromessaging.

---

[2] From a report by Deborah Dagit, Executive Director, Diversity and Workplace Environment at Merck USA.

Here is your first lesson: When someone accuses you of a microinequity, never respond with a statement—always with a question. Defensive statements, such as "That wasn't a microinequity, You misunderstood, or You're overreacting," set the framework for an adversarial discussion. Ask questions to understand how and why the other person felt the slight.

Even before I began my research and work on this topic, I attempted to discuss my perceptions with the manager I described earlier, putting my feelings on the table. Her response was predictable, "You're overreacting. Don't be so sensitive. You should focus your attention on the project not on what my eyes do. Puhleeeze!"

Of course, had she responded with a question, life for me might have been very different. Her response could have been: "What did you observe? Was that the first time you noticed this? How do I act differently to you? Why haven't you told me about this before?" What an amazing catalyst for change it would have been. She may not have agreed with my accusations, but exploring why I felt that way could have prompted a fruitful discussion. Instead, her statements shut down any chance of a two-way conversation.

Questions are far more effective than defensive statements. They do not imply agreement, but they do convey interest and a desire to understand and facilitate an environment for peak performance, a central thread of effective leadership. Give it a try.

The next time someone accuses you of virtually anything, ask some questions. Resolving the situation may take more time, but the outcome will likely be more productive for both of you.

Understanding how to identify and master micromessages in the workplace has the potential to spark a revolution in how the corporate world operates. Welcome to this new age of leadership.

CHAPTER 2

Micromessages: The DNA of Leadership

Don't make the mistake of confusing authority with leadership. Being the boss doesn't make you a leader. There is little correlation between the trappings of power and the ability to lead and inspire others.

You can have the impressive title, the cushy corner office, the power to direct others, even the perfect wardrobe, but those only dub you with authority. In reality, labels of authority have nothing to do with whether others consider you a leader or whether they'd be motivated to follow you. Unfortunately, people are often given the "power seat" to control the careers of others for reasons that have little to do with possessing the requisite skills. Top performers are typically rewarded with promotions into leadership positions for which they are unqualified.

> *Labels of authority have nothing to do with whether others consider you a leader or whether they'd be motivated to follow you.*

What a dilemma! But how else can you reward employees who do outstanding work if not by endowing them with more power? Bonuses and compensation are nice appeasements, but they do not convey stature. So companies bestow on their top performers greater responsibility and authority as an indication of their value to the organization and everyone is happy—except those who end up working for the new boss. The new bosses are often expected to learn through trial and error the skills of providing guidance, development, and direction. Unfortunately, people's lives and careers are often put at risk in order to provide leadership development training to a rising star.

Inspiring Others

So what are the most crucial leadership skills and how can you acquire them? Having a wealth of knowledge merely makes you a database. Knowing how to get things done only means you are connected. And having the power to make others do your bidding makes you little more then a dictator. The heart and soul of effective leadership is the means by which we motivate, inspire, and drive others to live up to their full potential. Moreover, the only way that inspiration, motivation, and drive are communicated is by the way the appropriate messages are sent.

It's not so much what we *say* that matters, but what the other person ends up *hearing* or inferring. We may think we're sending the exact same message to two team members, but the message they each receive may be very different and is affected by the nature of the relationship. Personal feelings (likes and dislikes) about each team member influence how we shape words, gestures, tone, inflection, and so many other aspects of the ways messages are transmitted. Even if we were able to send a message in an identical manner to two people (as impossible as that may be), the filter of the receiver uniquely influences the interpretation.

> The heart and soul of effective leadership is the means by which we motivate, inspire, and drive others to live up to their full potential.

Almost imperceptible subtleties of sending and receiving messages define micromessaging and its power of influence. These micromessages tell us how much we are valued and respected by those who control our destiny in the workplace. Micromessages tell us exactly where we stand and how far we are likely to go. They are as intangible as the medium through which they are sent. But, through them, we build loyalty or contempt, commitment or indifference, even inspiration or sabotage. Micromessages are the very soul of leadership, and leadership is the primary driver of performance.

Top 5 Obstacles Inhibiting Leadership Evolution

Immediately following one of my seminars, two university professors approached me to discuss a study they were currently working on. The study was focused on identifying the Top 5 obstacles inhibiting leadership evolution. Although the study is still ongoing, they have concluded that the number one obstacle inhibiting leadership evolution is *Ego*.

To make the point that it is far and away the number one inhibitor, they've chosen not to number the other four! A critical message is that we make many bad decisions and poor choices influenced by the need to save face. Basically, we are often more driven to be right than we are to seek truth.

Another key obstacle they cited is *Operating in the Ill-Defined*. In the workplace, we tend to use countless expressions that are blindly accepted and people walk away thinking, "I've got it." All too often, however, the exact meaning is unclear and we don't actually, "got it."

Here are just a few examples of expressions that are blindly tossed about in the workplace:

Think Outside of the Box
Be a Team Player
I Have Your Back

Let's look at how amorphous these expressions actually are.

Think Outside of the Box

I had a boss who would frequently say, in an effort to give us all his great insight, *"You need to think outside of the box."*

What the heck does that really mean? We all know that it generally implies doing things differently. But is that all I need to do to be an *outside of the box* thinker? Shouldn't there be some qualitative component connected with that expectation and what would that be? Would I not be thinking outside of the box until it was later confirmed that my *different* approach had succeeded? Or am I a good *outside of the box* thinker simply because others agreed with my new approach?

Although he directed me to think *outside of the box*, I'll betcha there was also *another* box, outside of *that* box, that I'd better NOT think outside of!

Back then, I just accepted this ill-defined direction, walking away thinking that I clearly knew what was expected, when in truth I had no clear understanding of what it was and, more importantly, what it would look like if done well.

Be a Team Player

To be a good team player do I need to agree with my teammates? Am I expected to cheer them on even when I disagree with their choices? More importantly, what are the actual behaviors I need to demonstrate to be doing *teamwork* well?

I Have Your Back

In a public forum on race relations, Lt. Governor Dan Patrick of Texas, while addressing President Obama said, "The police just want to know that you have their backs."

President Obama went on to explain that he did "have their backs" but no one in that public forum took the time to define what that expression actually meant and what it would look like if done well.

Does "having your back" mean covering for you when you've done something wrong? Does it mean protecting you at all costs?

I was challenged by a colleague when I raised this question. He said, "Steve, think about whether you have your children's backs and it would basically mean the same thing."

My response took the discussion to a much deeper level. I replied, "If having my children's backs means covering for them when they've broken the law, or closing ranks around the family to protect them when they've done something illegal, or writing a school note fabricating a tale to keep them out of trouble, then I don't have their backs. I expect them to demonstrate integrity and be responsible for their actions and accountable for their misdeeds." I continued, "I will always have their backs in providing love and financial support, but will not misrepresent the facts or unfairly conspire or cover for them."

Clearly, Lt. Gov. Patrick was not suggesting that President Obama provide love and personal financial support. So, in this example, what did "have their backs" really mean and what would it look like?

Business cultures tend to use expressions such as these and we blindly nod with understanding and acceptance when in fact, if challenged, each person will likely have a very different understanding of what it means and what it would look like if done well.

In addition to Ego and Operating in the Ill-Defined, another obstacle the professors identified as inhibiting leadership evolution is *Task Completion*.

They contend that when a person takes a job they are either provided a list, or create one for themselves, that defines doing the job "correctly." The paradox here is that Task Completion often becomes an obstacle or inhibitor because completing the items on that checklist tends to limit our leadership impact. We tend to limit our focus on technical completion of the tasks alone, such as:

- I greeted everyone on the team this morning (check!)
- I gave rich feedback to both the men and women (check!)
- I introduced the folks I was with to a respected colleague (check!)

Although done technically correctly, we often convey different levels of respect and engagement. We believe that we have done things well when, in fact, we've only done them correctly.

We must learn to identify our micromessages and apply them well, without being false or pretentious. In doing so, we greatly alter the loyalty and engagement of those with whom we work and, most importantly, influence their workplace performance.

One of the most common microinequities occurs when a manager introduces team members to a peer. Say there's a gathering of employees at a company event. You are the manager and have two of your direct reports standing with you. As you glance over you catch the eye of a colleague who is also a close friend. You approach, greet, and exchange a few pleasantries and, of course, introduce your team members. This is how it goes:

"Susan, let me introduce you to couple of people on my team." You flip your thumb to the left, where Adam is standing saying, "This is Adam. He is responsible for developing the course curriculum for the client training project." While speaking, your voice is flat and monotone. You don't look at Adam or

> *Micromessages are the very soul of leadership, and leadership is the primary driver of performance.*

Susan. You start clicking the pen you're holding and discreetly glance down at your watch. You continue, "It's also his responsibility to get the program distributed to all of our sites globally." Throughout the introduction your facial expression is appropriate but neutral, gazing down, off to the side, and occasionally at Susan.

Then you begin your introduction of Bill, turning your head to look directly at him, saying to Susan, "This is Bill!" In the short delivery of those three words, the tone of your voice is exuberant, lifted, and proud. "You know all those exciting speaker-series programs people have been getting all fired up about? Well, Bill here is the creative juice behind all that." You casually ask Susan if she has ever attended one of those programs. She nods and replies, "Yes, it was very informative." Beaming, you respond, "Well, Bill's the guy who put it all together."

Nearly everyone has been on both sides of that introduction; it's an all too common scenario. You've probably even played the role of that manager at some point.

It is unlikely the manager was aware of the difference in the introductions. It's also unlikely that the manager knowingly intended to treat the two employees differently, but *intent* plays a relatively small role in the damaging effects of microinequities. The microinequities reveal our true feelings. Unfortunately, we rarely step up to the underlying causes driving our feelings of dislike toward others. Adam can't walk away from that exchange with anything actionable. At best, he walks away puzzled about why he isn't valued. At worst, he is very clear about not respecting the manager and will turn on him the first chance he gets.

As for Bill, he's just comfortable basking in the glow of his manager's praise or empathetically embarrassed for Adam. Adam, no doubt, walks away knowing he's clearly not the favored child but is probably not able to put his finger on exactly what really occurred. What precisely was different? There were six crucial differences:

Facial Expression

The facial expression for Adam was expressionless and indifferent. For Bill, there was a bright sparkle of pride.

Tone of Voice

While the tone of the introduction for Bill could be chartered as musical notes on a score, Adam's sounded more like the flat-line pitch of an emergency room heart monitor.

Hand Gestures

While speaking of Bill, the manager's hand gestures occasionally pointed toward him (that's my boy), but the hands were fidgety or squarely resting in their pockets throughout Adam's introduction.

Choice of Words

As for the words, there was a matter-of-fact description for Adam, versus words of passion and pride for Bill. Adam's introduction was a résumé; Bill's was a review—and a four-star one at that.

Eye Contact

The manager couldn't help but turn and gaze proudly at Bill while talking about him, yet he never once looked at Adam. It's nearly impossible to avoid making eye contact with a person whom you are proudly introducing, but it is quite common to evade the eyes of a person you don't like or respect. You may not be conscious of what you're doing, but the message is clear.

Questions and Interaction

In this introduction, the manager asked Susan a question as a part of Bill's introduction. The manager asked Susan if she had ever attended one of Bill's programs. This makes Susan no longer a passive listener, but an active participant in Bill's introduction.

Unfortunately, the manager's different styles of introduction could never be cited or made a topic of discussion. What exactly would you point out to your manager? Can you imagine how much of a total sniveling whiner Adam would appear to be if he attempted to talk about any of this with his manager? "Do you have a minute, boss?" Adam might ask. "I'd like to talk to you about how you introduced me to Susan. I noticed you didn't smile and your choice of words seemed a bit flat and emotionless. You never pointed in my direction while talking about me. Oh, and your eyes didn't connect with mine."

Odds are the manager wouldn't recognize his error and apologize profusely. It's more likely he would take Adam by the arm and quietly escort him to the Employee Assistance Program Office for psychiatric care and be reminded why he didn't like Adam in the first place.

Without a deep understanding of how influential these micromessages can be, there is little Adam, or you, can do to get the manager to see and feel the impact of his behavior on loyalty and performance.

Separately, any of these micromessages seem petty but no one observing those introductions would have even the slightest confusion as to which subordinate was valued more.

Adam is made to feel unappreciated and on the outside. And there is a residual effect as well. When Adam and Bill interview with Susan for a job opportunity, Susan will never remember exactly why, but her admiration and respect for the manager will

> ## Balance Introductions
>
> When making introductions, pay careful attention to:
>
> - Facial expression
> - Tone of voice
> - Hand gestures
> - Choice of words
> - Eye contact
> - Questions/interaction

cause her to have an instant preference for Bill. Although micromessages quickly dissipate from memory, their influence can be indelible. They are the sort of weed in which, even when all visible signs are removed from the surface, the roots grow deep and insidious.

Maintaining an awareness of these six specific behaviors associated with micromessages is relatively easy. It's also extremely effective. That's not to say you should do anything pretentious or behave insincerely, but be aware that subtle behaviors can significantly shape the message you send to and about someone during a personal introduction, or virtually any dialogue.

Micromessages reveal what we really feel and carry powerful clues as to what exists between the lines. Law enforcement agencies have long focused on micromessages to get to the "truth" in their interviews and interrogations of suspects, witnesses, and victims. The Reid Technique of Interviewing and Interrogation, as developed by John E. Reid & Associates, Inc., incorporates careful observation of body posture, gestures, facial expressions, eye contact, even changes in facial color, when evaluating truth or deception during interviews and interrogations. These micromessages help agents sort truth from fiction. These same techniques can be used in the workplace and in personal relationships to expose pandering or to confirm sincerity.

> *Micromessages reveal what we really feel and carry powerful clues as to what exists between the lines.*

Starting Out on the Right Foot

Imagine it's your first day at your new job. You have just completed the company's orientation program, so you head to your work area to meet with your new manager. You feel an undertone of having made the wrong employment decision although he does nothing you could complain about, and certainly nothing even remotely indictable. Nevertheless, the following encounter taints your vision of him, the work environment, and the company, forever—at least as long as you are willing to stay.

The orientation program took half the day and when you arrive at your work area, it is about one o'clock. You approach the manager who is engaged in conversation with another employee. You are the model of bright-eyed and bushy-tailed as you wait your turn to connect with your new boss. He sees you, raises his palm in a way to suggest, "I'll be with you in a moment." You don't mean to eavesdrop, but you notice the conversation has shifted from business to idle social chatter. The banter continues and in an effort to be unobtrusive, you become a chameleon, blending into the background so as not to appear pushy.

Finally their conversation winds down, and they begin walking down the corridor. In his peripheral vision your manager is reminded that you're still there. He stops and tells the person he's with, "Hold on, it will just be a few moments, I need to talk to the new guy." "New Guy?" You begin to wonder how long that nickname will be pinned to your forehead.

He is appropriately polite—reaches his hand out, welcomes you, then tells you to follow him to the conference room for a team meeting about to begin. You think to yourself, "Wow, it's a good thing I decided not to have lunch and returned to the office right after the orientation," since no one told you about the team meeting.

The meeting begins and your manager starts off making you feel welcome. He introduces you to the team saying, "Everyone, please welcome our new team member, Robert Collins." He lets them know about your new role: "Robert is the team's new junior analyst, starting today." Everyone responds in a soft chorus of "Hello." He graciously closes your introduction with a very generous, "Robert, if you need anything, my door is always open."

During the meeting, your manager does nothing anyone would characterize as negative, but he never makes eye contact with you, doesn't ask your opinion, and when you offer an idea, his smirky smile silently implies, "Hurry up, kid, so we can get back to business."

Strolling back to your work area, you ask him where your workspace will be. He confidently replies, "We've been working on that and haven't quite finalized the details. I'm pretty sure one of those two desks over there is available. Why don't you settle in there for now?" Just before turning and walking away he adds, "Oh, and if you need any supplies or office stuff, see Marilyn."

That probably didn't seem so bad, right? After all, your boss took time from the team meeting to introduce you, your new colleagues were all polite and welcoming, and your manager even listened to your suggestion. As far as workspace, the manager's a busy guy and it's understandable that he wasn't able to pull the details together before your start date. And, you think to yourself, "I'm sure I'll be able to track down this Marilyn, whoever she is." That's one way to welcome a new employee, but let's rewind. Contrast that with the approach of an enlightened manager who has been exposed to the influence of micromessaging.

This manager sends an overnight package to the new employee's home welcoming him a few days in advance of his start date and outlining key events for the upcoming week, including a team meeting scheduled for early afternoon of his first day. The manager anticipates the time she expects the new hire will arrive after orientation and schedules a brief meeting to get him oriented. In addition, she makes sure his desk is fully stocked with all the necessary office supplies in advance of his arrival. When he arrives after the orientation, she is waiting and they have a private chat during which the employee gets the opportunity to ask basic questions. They walk to the team meeting together and she begins with a welcome and a brief summary of Robert's background, interests, and role.

She invites Robert to participate in the meeting, asking him, "I know you're not familiar with all the details of this project but do you have any thoughts on which approach might work best?" During the rest of the day, at the request of their manager, each team member stops by the new employee's desk to reintroduce themselves and to chat for a few minutes about how they might work together on upcoming projects. At the end of the day, the manager stops back to check in on her employee. "So, how was your first day?" She asks with a warm smile. Not surprisingly, she is told, "In just a day, I feel like I have a really good understanding of what everyone does and how I fit in. At other companies, it's taken weeks to get to this point and sometimes it's like pulling teeth."

Microadvantages, positive micromessages, can have a big impact on employee performance, commitment, loyalty, and output.

Imagine the contribution that new employee will make in the coming weeks and years. The difference between these two experiences comes down to *microadvantages*. Microadvantages, positive micromessages, can have a big impact on employee performance, commitment, loyalty, and output.

A number of years ago, in my former role as a corporate middle manager, the head of my division, John, would, once or twice a year, spot me passing by his office and call to me by name, inviting me in to chat. After the initial superficial chitchat, the subject would turn to my family: He'd refer to my wife by first name and ask how my son and daughter were doing in school. He'd also reveal a few personal details about himself, such as a story about his own daughter at college. The conversation didn't last more than five minutes—ten at most—but at no time during the conversation did he ever ask about the status of a report, details about a project, or anything else that was business-related. The conversation was exclusively about me—and him.

Maximize the Power of First Impressions

The old cliché about first impressions is true but incomplete. First impressions are more than lasting; they are indelible and set the stage for the productivity and quality of every relationship. As a leader, how you set the stage of a new employee's first day directly influences the productivity and success of that individual and his contributions to your team over the long term.

He could just as easily have incorporated any number of business items into the discussion, but instead chose to make the conversation personal, building my commitment and loyalty. I wasn't just another employee, I was in the inner circle—or at least I felt that way—and frankly, that was all that mattered.

John's simple and subtle actions were signs of great leadership. The micromessages he sent caused me to become one of his biggest supporters. There was no task he could assign that I wasn't thrilled to take on. His requests came first and nothing would prevent me from working 100 percent on his behalf. And if anyone even thought about bad-mouthing or gossiping about him, I would become a pit bull in his defense. In just a few minutes, with no more than a handful of questions, John created a powerful relationship that certainly benefited my career *and* his.

There are also managers who inspire quite the opposite reaction and relationship. One person summed the differences in her feelings about her former and current manager this way: "If I looked out the window and saw my former manager walking toward an open manhole, I would spring from my desk and do whatever was humanly possible to save him—including risking my own hide. If I saw my current manager walking toward that manhole, I'd likely spin around in my chair and look the other way, hoping he'd fall in."

I'm sure you know the feeling. Everyone has worked for that *other* kind of boss at some point in his or her career. That feeling—whether you'll save them or let them self-destruct—does not originate in the part of our brain where right and wrong are decided; it is fueled by emotion.

Communication Disconnects

If you are a boss, how many of your subordinates would leap to your defense if it weren't explicitly part of their job description? This is the reason many managers "fall down the manhole." Of course, managers can have those same kinds of feelings about their subordinates as well. Micromessages influence relationships both up and down the corporate ladder; they are not the sole property of managers and leaders. Micromessages shape every kind of relationship, giving bosses and workers equal opportunity to either damage a relationship or forge a better working relationship.

Just as you instinctively know how your boss feels about you, she also senses how you feel about her. Though neither of you may be aware of the messages being sent, the recipient unwittingly under-stands the micromessages and reacts accordingly. Once we've had the time to learn an individual style and behavior, the accuracy of our interpretation of the person's micromessages improves. Some learn faster than others.

A woman made a point of telling me about one of those excep-tions during one of my seminars. She asked why so many men she had dated seemed to have what resembled a form of Asperger's syn-drome (a disconnect in the way micromessages are understood and interpreted). People with severe Asperger's syndrome cannot discern the meanings of facial expressions. They are unable to distinguish the difference between a smile, a frown, a raised eyebrow of uncer-tainty, or a nod of agreement. This condition was precisely what she felt was going on with several of her blind dates! She described how, during one date, she gave every micromessage imaginable to get the evening to come to an early end, but nothing got through. She yawned, sighed, checked her watch, never smiled, let her eyes wander, and even talked about missing her old boyfriend, just about everything short of saying, "If you were the last person on earth ... this would still be our last date."

Micromessages shape every kind of relationship, giving bosses and workers equal opportunity to either damage a relationship or forge a better working relationship.

When the evening ended, she felt they had been in parallel uni-verses. He smiled and said, "Wow, I had a great time. I think we really hit it off. How about getting together again tomorrow night?" "Is this why they call it a 'blind date?" she asked. "How could any-body be so oblivious to all my signals?" she wondered. Are some people just not as attuned to reading micromessages as others? Or does persistence just take over and make some people blind to any-thing that gets in their way?

Asperger's aside, there *are* some people who read micromessages better than others. For communicating better with her "blind date" she might have considered going back to our earlier discussion in the Introduction about asking questions. She might have asked, "What do you think makes people compatible?"or "What do you look for when deciding if someone's having a good evening?" Then perhaps he would have clued in to the message he should have been receiving all along.

It does seem that men tend to be less attuned to micromessage decoding than women; however, everyone can learn to recognize and manage the sending and receiving of micromessages. Dr. Mary Rowe's pioneering research, discussed earlier in our introduction,[1] uncovered how these subtle and, in some cases, near invisible, messages are infinitely more powerful and far more pervasive than any of the large, discriminatory behavior we pretty much have under control in the workplace.

Dr. Rowe first began to explore unspoken communication as it affected students in 1973. She examined how the way someone raises or lowers his voice, smiles or does not smile, affected interactions. We receive a micromessage when someone makes eye contact or looks away, from the way a person coolly or warmly greets a staffer or fails to do so altogether. A micromessage can

> *Micromessages reveal what is behind our masks, including hidden assumptions that connect underachievement in the workplace with race, gender, nationality, religious preference, class, and appearance.*

be sent in a dismissive hand gesture, a positioning of the body toward or away from someone who is speaking; it can be the movement of a leg on a sofa that does not allow someone to join

---

[1] Rowe, "Barriers to Equality," 1990.

a group; it can be in the tone of a flat, emotionless phone message or a cryptic e-mail.

In the case of my old boss, John, the micromessages of care, respect, trust, and inclusion were conveyed. Those easily delivered messages made me work harder for him, created unconditional loyalty, unlocked any inhibitions to my creativity, and sparked a genuine desire to make the company more successful.

Dr. Rowe discovered that for some, sending small snubs can be reflexive habits and the product of cultural conditioning that begins at birth. Micromessages reveal what is behind our masks, including hidden assumptions that connect underachievement in the workplace with race, gender, nationality, religious preference, class, and appearance.

These messages are called "micro" not because you can't easily see them but because they seem insignificant; their impact, however, is nothing short of monumental. On the surface, they're hardly worth talking about; they are the sort of thing that would leave you appearing to be hypersensitive and overemotional should you raise them as an issue.

By the time Dr. Rowe published her groundbreaking white paper in 1990, outright discriminatory attitudes and their accompanying behavior—*macro*inequities—were close to being invisible in the business environment. She had done nearly twenty years of research, detecting the prevalence of microinequities in the work environment at a time when they truly were macro.

The insults were direct, the language blatant, and the prevalence widespread. Fast-forward twenty years and the outright expressions of discriminatory attitudes have been all but banished from the workplace. However, many of the sentiments have not disappeared—they've just gone underground. From beneath the surface, they come back to do their damage in the form of microinequities. While they are less blatant and hard-hitting, microinequities are perhaps more insidious because of their ephemeral nature. The negative impact of micromessages builds up over time, hampering performance, and even causing emotional maladjustment. Not unlike Jonathan Swift's Gulliver, some of us wake to find ourselves tied to the ground by those very things we barely see and didn't take seriously.

> *The negative impact of micromessages builds up over time, hampering performance, and even causing emotional maladjustment.*

It's like worrying about the elephants while the ants walk by. Corporate policies and laws have done a great job controlling the big and visible behaviors that send destructive messages (the metaphorical elephant), but we are overrun by billions of ants that we barely notice. It is these subtle micromessages that drive everything about how relationships operate. They are literally everywhere and occur at all times. Micromessages operate at all levels of power, sent downward by managers, upward by subordinates, and laterally by colleagues.

Much of our behavior is simply what makes us human. We tend to find comfort in commonality. Leaders as well seem to be more effective at developing people who are like themselves. In addition to preferring an individual based on race, gender, or age, consciously or subconsciously, they are also influenced by personal style, class, religious choice, political views, and more. In fact, before we make an effort to speak with someone, we pass people through a series of filters, searching for similar traits and styles. It's how we decide whether to let them into our inner circle.

> *Micromessages operate at all levels of power, sent downward by managers, upward by subordinates, and laterally by colleagues.*

Stage one of this process includes asking: How are you like me? Do we look alike? Are we close in age? Do we have the same social background? Do we share a similar ethnic culture? Did you attend a school in my league? What is your social standing? What is your nationality?

When there aren't enough common factors in stage one, people rarely delve any further and lose interest in pursuing a connection. We search for indicators, real or otherwise, to validate keeping our distance. Yet commonalities can also create distance, especially when a manager seems to be giving preferential treatment to a subordinate, which is what happened to Peter in the story that follows.

An Example of Mixed Micromessages

Peter began working at a Fortune 500 company where the CEO, Roger, was one of his father's closest friends. Because of that personal connection, Roger regularly stopped by Peter's cubicle to see how he was doing. And naturally Peter learned about the company at an accelerated pace, surpassing the other new hires and earning their disdain. But he never made the connection between his casual comments about weekend dinners with his Dad and the CEO at the club, and the polite coolness from nearly everyone on the team. No one would socialize with him, and when they did converse with him, his colleagues were clearly guarded about sharing information.

Peter sensed something was wrong. When he tried talking to his coworkers, they assured him by their words that everything was fine, but everything didn't feel fine to Peter. He couldn't put his finger on it, but the microinequities were coming from every angle nonstop—and they weren't good.

Peter turned to his father, whose extensive business experience usually provided good perspective for piecing things together. His father reacted with emotion, not logic, and went straight to his old friend Roger to talk about how his son was being excluded by his coworkers. He suggested that Roger try to fix the problem.

The message was swift and clear: Everyone quickly understood they were to be nicer to Peter. Unfortunately, and predictably, the directive had the opposite effect. On the surface everything changed. Now everyone made it their business to seek Peter out and say: "Good morning, Peter. How was your weekend, Peter? Is there anything I can do for you, Peter?" However, they did this in an exaggerated, phony, in-your-face, purposeful way. If Peter felt isolated before, he was now on an uncharted island. There was little he could complain about. Everyone was doing exactly what they were *supposed* to do, but he felt even more ostracized than before.

> *Understanding the behaviors that underlie micromessages will dramatically increase your ability to control them, but total fluency will probably always be just beyond your grasp, as it is for all of us.*

It was all quite obvious, but Peter felt limited in what he could say or do since everyone was, at least in their macromessages, so proper and polite. There was nothing he could do. He lacked the ability to define and, more importantly, to confront and resolve the microinequities.

He initially believed his association with the CEO would spark others to be drawn to him. But Peter was unaware of a cornerstone of office politics: Those with genuine power are magnetic—but those simply holding the robes of power are powerless and only create jealousy and envy when they flaunt their connections. Peter was dangerously unaware of the micromesages *he* had been sending his colleagues.

He believed he had special status, and the message he was sending was, "I have access to the inner sanctum. I can help you. Treat me like I'm special and my specialness will rub off on you and your career as well." But that's not the message his coworkers received at all. They perceived that he was receiving unfair preferential treatment because of his father's friendship with their boss, and they didn't appreciate his expectation of fawning attention.

The unilateral reprimand to the staff regarding Peter confirmed their perception and the microinequities began. However, they continued to follow a fundamental rule: As long as you *say* the right thing, no one can come back and challenge you. They were right. Peter was stymied.

Understanding the behaviors that underlie micromessages will dramatically increase your ability to control them, but total fluency will probably always be just beyond your grasp, as it is for all of us. Millions of years of mammalian behavior drives us to react by envy, fear, jealousy, anger, greed, love, and countless emotions and instinct, which can be toxic to the effective building of relationships of all types.

Begin with Introspection

You are never immune from being a perpetrator. When you sense tension, resistance, distrust, or other symptoms of distance, begin with introspection. What am I doing that may be causing what I am experiencing? Ask questions about your own behavior and you are likely to uncover what would otherwise remain undercover.

The more you practice the art of micromessaging, the more you will discover how its mastery lies at the center of effective leadership and forms the foundation of individual performance. It's a fact: Micromessaging is hardwired to your businesses' bottom line. Positive micromessaging can energize employee engagement and impact financial performance for the better. A September 2005 survey conducted by Towers Perrin and research conducted by Richard S. Wellins in an April 2005 *Workforce Performance Solutions*

Magazine article demonstrate just how far this can trickle right down to your businesses' bottom line.[2]

Forty-one global companies, classified into high- or low-engagement work environments, were evaluated over the course of thirty-six months to determine what impact employee engagement had on business performance. The results were clear. High-engagement companies showed positive financial gains, while low-engagement companies posted losses.

Leaders cannot be at their most effective until they learn to read, analyze, and respond to the micromessages that have been in their blind spot. You must become aware of the power that sending these messages has on everyone around you. As a leader, you can inspire commitment, engagement, and embolden creativity through something as micro and simple as the way you begin your workday—with how you say "Hello." It's in the DNA of what makes great leaders great.

> *Leaders cannot be at their most effective until they learn to read, analyze, and respond to the micromessages that have been in their blind spot.*

2 Richard S. Wellins and James Concelman, "Creating a Culture for Engagement," *Workforce Solutions Magazine*, April 2005; Towers Perrin. "Senior Leaders Improve Their Communication," white paper/press release, Stamford CT: Towers Perrin Communications Consortium, September 7, 2005.

CHAPTER 3

Don't Label Me—
Learn Me

A great deal of emphasis has been placed on examining and managing our generational differences, particularly in the workplace. We've learned that there tend to be differences in the ways Millennials communicate in contrast with the ways the "GenXers" or "Baby Boomers" choose to send their messages. The differences abound.

Learning about these traits is eye-opening, but how should we use this knowledge to make the workplace function more effectively? Interestingly, the concept of labeling has long carried a negative connotation. At one time, labeling and stereotyping were virtually synonyms.

Racial profiling has never been sanctioned and remains a call-to-arms when we see such behavior exhibited by law enforcement, the TSA, or in our schools. Labeling or stereotyping is universally considered a virtual axiom of pejorative behavior.

With this as our axiom, how then can we sanction a new form of social labeling in our current Diversity & Inclusion education programs? Consider, instead, a new model that acknowledges the differences, but doesn't establish labels of behavior that cause us to paint any group that shares that difference with a broad brush.

I recall, many years ago, my company required all managers to take a Myers-Briggs Personality Type Indicator questionnaire.

Myers-Briggs is an introspective, self-report designed to indicate psychological preference in the ways we perceive our surroundings and make decisions. It assesses four principal psychological functions—sensation, intuition, feeling, and thinking—through a series of 93 questions. After dutifully filling out the questionnaire and submitting my responses, it generated the analytics that confined me to a four-letter code (ESTJ) based on the answers I provided.

The history of how these tests were developed dates back to the eighteenth century when head-shape was actually used to categorize and predict personality. In the more recent era, personality tests were used by the U.S. Military in the 1920s. The armed forces used these personality "type indicators" as a tool for personnel assignments to place soldiers in the jobs for which they would be best suited.

These psychological tests are all based on Carl Jung's study of psychological traits. His work analyzed the following *Big Five* personality trait categories; mind, energy, nature, tactics, and identity. Using today's corporate version of personality profiling, people are typed as:

- Extroversion vs. Introversion
- Sensing vs. Intuition
- Thinking vs. Feeling
- Judging vs. Perceiving

I paraded my "ESTJ" profile with the near pride of having received a special achievement award! Many of my colleagues crafted small tent cards with their Type Indicator four-letter code and placed them prominently on their desks for all to see.

How enlightened we all felt that we could walk into someone's office and know exactly who they were and subsequently how we should treat them!

In reality, that enlightenment was a pernicious mask of misperception. I may have been a certain type of communicator on the day I took the profiling test, but on a different day, speaking with a different set of colleagues, against a different deadline, on a topic I was less familiar with, it would likely have dramatically changed that four-letter code.

It is true, certain styles may represent how we generally function in a majority of workplace situations, but these predictors are insufficient. They cannot effectively guide us in the ways we should treat people. Certainly 93 questions, or any number of static data points, should not shape how we assess and interact with those in the workplace. This kind of labeling process is more likely to inhibit performance than advance it.

Stereotyping has never been sanctioned as an appropriate way to assess groups of people. Yet somehow, this personality testing process gained credibility although it was nothing more than another form of profiling and stereotyping structured with a different set of data.

Let's take a step forward and look at a more current workplace practice that has reinvented the stereotyping process. Analyzing the behaviors and traits of generational group differences has become a popular area of focus as we strive to be more culturally inclusive. We've moved from four-letter "Type Indicators" to broader generational and other designators; GenZ, Millennials, GenX, Baby Boomers, LGBTQ, et al.

There are times I behave like a traditional Baby Boomer, but under different conditions with different audiences and different demands and expectations, I might appear more like a GenX or even a Millennial. When you give it careful thought, what is the purpose and, more importantly, applicable value in having this profile information? What should we do with it in the ways we interact with our colleagues in the workplace?

Here is a perfect example that demonstrates the dangers of generational labeling. My mother, an elderly woman in her eighties, would certainly not be expected to fit the profile of a Millennial. But when you look at her style of communicating, you would quickly learn that she loves her iPad and prefers texting to talking— probably because she's just a grouchy old lady.

Her tablet dings constantly with text notifications because people know she's not going to answer their phone calls (she hates telephones). She'll raise her half-inch-thick reading glasses and, with those giant eyes, screen all her text messages. She might respond immediately or decide, based on a variety of factors, to flip the tablet to the side as she mentally flips the sender to the side along with it.

Also out of character to her generational profile, she feels the rules don't apply to her!

Contrast my mom with my Millennial daughter who, of course, texts messages all the time. But after two or three exchanges, she's likely to pick up the phone, give me a call, and talk about the topic at hand.

If one were to use the so-called wisdom we gain by profiling a generational group, you'd be dead wrong for both my mother and my daughter.

This is one of the fundamental flaws of generational profiling in the workplace. If you were to discover that I was an "ESTJ" or, in current workplace focus, a Baby Boomer, male, African American and used any of the profiling data to determine how best to communicate with me, you would greatly miss the mark.

We must instead focus on learning the individual and not the category with which the individual is labeled. The primary goal is to motivate and inspire the performance of all those with whom we work—in other words, *don't label me, learn me.*

Labeling can also inhibit the progress of disenfranchised groups and ethnicities. I was invited to speak at a women's conference in

Finland for the technology industry. Admittedly, this did feel a little awkward. Here I was, an American male invited as the keynote speaker at a conference in Europe, whose focus was on the development of women.

One of my early remarks incited quite a reaction from many of the attendees. The provocative statement that set things off was my suggestion that one of the biggest inhibitors in addressing the needs of women in the workplace is focusing on *women*. How dare an American male (emphasis on American) come here and make such an outlandish remark! After all, wasn't that the purpose of the conference?

It didn't take long for them to begin to see the value of the statement and get fully on board with a new way of thinking.

I explained that placing the focus on any particular group tends to alienate those who are not a part of that group. Those who are not direct beneficiaries of the effort are likely to only do what they are told to do in compliance. Whenever they interact with the targeted group they are likely to execute the tasks in a somewhat mechanical manner and do so under duress.

It brought to mind a powerful conversation I had with a colleague at a Wall Street firm. A white investment banker and very close friend and I were having a conversation about our company's diversity progress.

Our company had won numerous national diversity awards and broad industry recognition for our work. After meeting with colleagues from other firms in the industry, I shared with my friend the frustration I was feeling after having learned that my company's work was really no better than many of the programs operating at other firms. It seemed the only difference was that I knew how to win awards.

Over our casual lunch, I asked him why he thought this was. He said something that made the hair on my back stand on end, but awakened me to a very different perspective.

He offered, "If you really want to get white guys to buy-in to this diversity thing, you have to take it out of the world of charity and good deeds. You have to make it something that genuinely causes them to connect and see the value in an area that they already respect." He continued, indicating that, if ever asked, he would never admit to saying these words, "Steve, when white guys hear the word diversity, their minds go to the Special Olympics."

I was getting more and more uncomfortable.

He continued, "They genuinely believe in their hearts that we need to help those poor disadvantaged folks, but don't try and convince me that they are really the top athletes because they're not. Until you get this out of that charitable arena and link it directly to something that those guys already believe has value, D&I will continue to remain a peripheral and obligatory effort driven by compliance."

He ended saying, "Basically, you have to get them to genuinely buy-in."

That conversation took my thinking to a place I had never imagined I would accept. As I developed the strategy to support that objective, I recognized that the old-fashioned approach that attempts to get buy-in by talking about the so-called business case for diversity was nothing more than a spoonful of sugar on top of some very unpleasant-tasting medicine.

Those majority white men were not buying into the rhetoric they were being fed to motivate their endorsement of D&I. They were hearing platitudes and clichés that sent echoes of—yada, yada, yada, help those people who have their problems, do good deeds, and more yada, yada, yada.

With the insight gleaned from my conversation came the critical need to find a way to link the mission of inclusion to something that everyone with high aspirations has embraced since their first day of work.

That link is *leadership*. There is nothing cliché or obligatory about wanting to be a great leader. Leadership is not determined by one's technical skills or one's ability to complete operational tasks.

Great leadership is solely determined by the ways in which we motivate and inspire others to perform. The only way this can be accomplished is through the messages we send. In most cases, it's not what we say, but what people hear that matters.

One can believe that I'm sending the same message to two people, but because of the nature of our relationships there are often subtle differences in the ways those subtle messages are sent.

Changing the manner in which we send our micromessages can directly impact the performance of those with whom we work, those who work for us, and most importantly, our relationships with clients and customers.

Unconscious Bias on the Public Stage

There is a critical need to shift the focus away from merely making people aware of unconscious bias data, the resulting bad behavior, and providing introspection on the cause. The new focus must be on getting leaders to buy-in to a new way of thinking because they clearly see the impact on how they become viewed, by everyone, as a better leader.

It was fascinating to watch two dimensions of unconscious bias play out on the public stage.

The South by Southwest Conference (SXSW) is an annual festival of film, interactive media, and music that takes place in Austin, Texas. The interactive media component has become a technology centerpiece that features many of the world's tech luminaries and is a popular international platform where senior executives come together and give their outlook and perspective on the future of the science and technology industries.

The 2015 SXSW conference highlighted a forum titled "How Innovation Happens," which featured three prominent panelists: Eric Schmidt, Google CEO; Megan Smith, United States Chief Technology Officer, former Google employee (notably, the panel's only woman); and Walter Isaacson, Steve Jobs's biographer and former CEO of CNN.

The panel discussion focused on how an increased level of diversity and gender inclusivity is necessary to bring about breakthroughs in the tech sphere—ironic considering the panel was all-white.

The panelists fielded several questions from the audience. Judith Williams, Google's diversity and inclusion executive, raised an interesting question—more a calling out than an actual request for information.

Ms. Williams observed that the two men had interrupted Ms. Smith repeatedly during the panel discussion. Williams said, "Given that unconscious bias research tells us that women are interrupted a lot more than men, I'm wondering if you are aware that you have interrupted Megan many more times." The crowd cheered at the comment and the program continued.

I am compelled to briefly digress and acknowledge the Google culture that allows an employee to openly call out the CEO on his bad behavior in front of colleagues and the general public.

In most of my corporate jobs, doing that sort of calling-out of the boss would certainly result in my personal belongings being packed and ready for me before returning to the office.

Here's the paradox. No doubt it was an emotionally inspiring moment for all the women in the audience who felt vindicated for the many times they were disrespected at all those meetings and presentations with similar interruptions. Certainly Eric Schmidt felt more aware of his offensive behavior and may likely never interrupt a woman in public again. But herein lies that paradox . . .

Eric Schmidt's focus may likely manage this newly acquired awareness by interacting differently with women. He will focus exclusively on changing his behavior when dealing with women. However, his intention may not be to focus on when interrupting is, versus is not, appropriate in *any* business setting.

He is more likely to single out women as a group he must respond to *differently* than operating in his normal process where he may interrupt when reasonable and appropriate.

He may elect to more tightly hold the reigns, bridling himself and remain restrained possibly thinking to himself, "I'm dealing with a woman. Let me keep my mouth shut and just let her finish."

That thinking process drives an attitude toward women that they are a sort of special needs group that one must handle with kid gloves and not conduct oneself in the ways that would be normal with other colleagues.

We believe the outcome is more effective when he is made to understand what interruptions do when they are not necessary. Whether interrupting a woman or one of the "good ole" boys, we must pay close attention to the impact we may be having on their respect for the speaker and how this kind of disruption impairs performance.

Eric Schmidt and other leaders should change their behavior because they have embraced the broader value of being an effective leader *all the time* and not speak to women differently as a special group. Speak with everyone in a way that builds their respect, loyalty, and ability to perform, regardless of gender, race, generational, or other differences.

Having people reach this level of understanding this concept and in turn, getting them to buy-in, becomes achievable once a person is guided through an experience where they can directly feel the effect on their own performance when micromessages are sent differently.

For example, it doesn't take long for a person to recognize that when your boss gives you feedback by saying, *Let me offer some suggestions that might help next time* versus, *Let me tell you what you did wrong,* there will be a considerable difference in the receptivity to the feedback.

I could hear from my boss say, all day; *Steve, let me offer some suggestions that might help next time.* On the other hand, I would just need to hear one time *Let me tell you what you did wrong* and I don't want to hear any more feedback.

This is just one of the countless examples that illustrate how sending messages differently, through our micromessages, can have a profound effect on someone's loyalty, commitment, motivation, and most critically, their performance. More importantly, these behaviors are also the criteria that are the determining factors of one's leadership impact.

I've watched the transformation countless times. Audiences of business professionals arrive at my seminar with a preconceived notion that the seminar they're about to attend will be about expectations and compliance regarding diversity and inclusion. In many cases I can almost hear them thinking, "This is a session about how I'm supposed to help someone, other than myself."

It doesn't take long to observe a dramatic shift in attitude once they're put through the process of feeling the direct impact micromessages have on their own performance.

They recognize that the people they have respected the most in the workplace are those who do this well.

Let's bring this back full circle to generational, gender, and other differences.

The power of leadership rests in one's fluency in speaking the language of influence and motivation. Micromessages are the heart and soul of great leadership and great leadership focuses on consistently sending effective, supporting, engaging messages to, well, *everyone*. Don't label me—learn me!

In the next chapter, you'll learn how to begin reading and sending micromessages before saying your first word.

CHAPTER 4

The Blind Spot

Have you ever observed how colleagues greet each other? Watch how they acknowledge one another and establish visual contact, how close they stand, and listened to the inflection of their words. At first glance, such greetings might appear to be repetitive, but when you take a closer look at the gestures, tone, inflection, and gazes you'll catch clues as to where everyone stands. You'll spot some relationships that are close and personal, and others that appear somewhat strained. Sometimes even without uttering a word the micromessages of a silent greeting can spell out who is, and who is not, "connected."

At work, watch the ways in which participants stroll into the conference room. You can bet people will greet each other politely, but even those polite greetings carry their own special signals.

Different Is Dangerous

The difference in how we greet others at meetings is rooted in ancestral tribal behaviors. Prehistoric humans were likely skilled at identifying the subtle visual differences of those from different tribes. We have no real proof, but I imagine that their daily mantra presumably reflected something like: "Unknown is unsafe; different is dangerous."

Even today, those words resonate in our behaviors. It is common to kill something that looks unusual or different out of fear. If it has a recognizable head, eyes that look into yours, four limbs, and utters comforting sounds, it gets to live another day. If it is unfamiliar, has antennae, six legs, bulging eyes, buzzes, and lands within arm's reach, a firmly rolled newspaper may be the last thing it feels.

In common is comforting, but different is dangerous. Young children instinctively gravitate to others of the same age. Little girls play with little girls, and boys with boys, until hormones drive changes in interest. And in the cafeterias of our most diverse schools, like kinds still sit in silos at lunch. We prefer to be with people with whom we have the most in common, whether it's age, gender, race, education, department, or authority figure.

Our natural drive pushes us to hone in on the characteristics of commonality. When confined with a group of strangers, we'll go pretty far to create a common bond where there's little more than a thin thread. I have been in meetings where two people uncover that they grew up in bordering towns and become fast friends. Let's see, bordering towns, 10 miles apart, at a meeting only three states away. Wow! Isn't that rare! Let's face it, there isn't much significance in having dined in a few of the same restaurants, or even having walked their dogs (probably a decade apart) in the same park, but such commonalities spark people to build a relationship that continues to grow well after the meeting's end.

What's wrong with catering to our natural social instincts that have been a part of us for millions of years? Quite frankly nothing, if we don't want to evolve. Today, we are predominantly urban-centered, nontribal beings. We are not confined to living in a 25-mile radius and we no longer drag a heavy club. We work on teams that extend beyond those we can reach within earshot, and have developed an interbred culture, leaving virtually no extended family "purebred." And we rely on more sophisticated messaging to communicate verbally and visually with those around us.

How we greet someone sets the stage for what is likely to follow. We sometimes delude ourselves into believing we have done everything right and, in truth, the surface messages are fine. The sender of the greeting may believe he is smiling, saying, and doing all the right things, while the micromessages originate from a different place of thought and communicate at a deeper level. The microinequities rear their ugly faces, and the chemistry goes haywire. The meeting goes on and we rarely process the nonverbal messages that we've received. More importantly, and more dangerously, we don't realize how these messages shape our own workplace identities.

How we greet someone sets the stage for what is likely to follow.

Greetings That Go Beyond the Obligatory

Greetings can have a profound impact on our relationships and leadership ability. To greet others effectively, it is necessary to shun clichéd words and gestures so commonly used in business meetings. Toss that customary greeting out the window; it's worthless if you aspire to be an authentic leader. For your greeting to inspire others and initiate a personal bond, it must include questions beyond the predictable "How are you?" or "How's it going?" To do that, ask about something personal but not intrusive, "Did that rainstorm last week hit your town?" or "How's your son doing at the university?"

Share something personal about yourself, "I'm considering one of those hybrid cars. What do you know about them?" or "I took the family to that new movie last weekend. Have you seen it?"

It can be particularly effective to greet someone making reference to something the person said the last time you were together. Your greeting will stand out as unique and leave a lasting impression.

In fact, recalling a comment or an idea the individual presented in a previous meeting is quite powerful. Imagine the effect when, after your initial greeting, you say, "In the last meeting you made a comment suggesting we reduce the number of items in the client survey. That was really a smart idea to put on the table."

It's easy to do this. At your next meeting, as a part of your routine note taking, record one or two of the comments each person offers. Whether you agree or not with the comment won't matter. It's only important that the comment was worthy of the group's discussion. In the margin next to each comment simply jot down that person's name.

Then, before the next meeting begins, scan the margin and review the comments from people who will be attending the meeting. Don't worry about recognizing everyone in the room; just choose a few. You can catch the other folks at subsequent meetings. You will be amazed at the outcome and, more importantly, they will be amazed with you. The impact of that minor acknowledgement could forge a quick and tight bond—with virtually no known solvent to pull it apart.

Visible Common Bonds

When the common elements people share are easily visible, the connection often happens with little effort. Familiarity, whether by gender, race, or circumstance, creates an immediate connection. When groups of like individuals are together, there are still plenty of subtle messages that announce any number of microinequities and microadvantages. People make eye contact; they perhaps offer a light smile, a nod, or a slight lift of the chin. And from this they know how close each is to the "inner circle." In those ten minutes or so of premeeting social chatter, everything about personal relationships is reconfirmed. Though never spoken, a careful observer could easily discern the rings of each concentric social circle. Don't be lulled into the belief that this is about being nice. Effective micromessaging isn't about doing the right thing. It is about identifying your proximity to the inner circle.

Don't Focus on Nice

It's easy to confuse the concepts of microadvantages with being kind or nice. Don't be mistaken. The heart and soul of effective micromessaging is really about inspiring self-esteem, commitment, loyalty, trust, and respect—the elements that separate management from leadership. And being in the inner circle has little to do with being nice.

Relativity Is Key

After about three years in one assignment, I was promoted to an exciting new role. The hiring manager had even personally encouraged me to apply for the position. On my first day in the new assignment, my new manager and I had a cozy chat to get to know each other. The conversation was cordial and respectful, and I knew he genuinely liked me because he had aggressively pursued me for months to join his team.

After the morning get-together and exchange of various documents, I left his office, went to my new cubicle, and began setting up my new digs. It couldn't have been more than twenty minutes when I heard a loud, booming bellow ringing from his office, "STEVE! GET IN HERE!" What could I have possibly done so badly in such a short time, I wondered.

I sheepishly walked into his office and was caught off-guard by his smile. He handed me a few additional documents he had misplaced during our earlier conversation and shared with me a few more details about the team. Apparently, I had done nothing wrong.

By the time I arrived back at my desk, all productivity ceased. I immediately began calling all my friends, whining about my obnoxious new boss and awful career move. Most of the conversations featured me repeating, "What a jerk. I've been here all of an hour and I'm being yelled at like a naughty child. If this is Day One, I can only imagine next week. What a big mistake I made. I never should have taken this job."

About thirty minutes later I heard another booming screech from his office, "SUSAN, UP AND IN HERE, NOW."

Then, a short while later, the walls shook again, this time with, "HARRY, YOU'RE OUT THERE. I'M IN HERE. YOU GET IN HERE!"

By mid-morning I learned the yelling was just his way of calling people, that's all. It's how he communicated. And realizing that I was being treated like everyone else on the team was actually comforting. Believe it or not, if he had yelled that way to all the people he liked, but didn't yell at me, my first day would really have been ruined. Had he screamed at my teammates and politely buzzed me on the phone to ask if I wouldn't mind stopping by, I would have felt like an outsider, not a member of the "in crowd." Recognizing that my new boss was not trying to be rude, or to send me a signal, I relaxed.

You can never determine whether a message is a microinequity or a microadvantage in a vacuum. It must be balanced against the way similar messages are delivered to others. Strangely enough, a punch on the arm can put you squarely in the inner circle, while customary politeness may place you on the outer fringes. Compare the micromessages you're receiving to what others in your circle are also receiving before making assumptions about their meaning.

Remaining Neutral

Sometimes the most effective way to send a neutral message is to remove the indicators of personal feelings. News agencies purport to be unbiased in their delivery of news to the public. This intent, whether genuine or not, is a rare journalistic reality.

Journalism typically presents news content in one of four categories: reportage, analysis, commentary, or editorialization. Reportage presents the pure facts; what happened, when it occurred, where it happened, and who was involved. Analysis brings the story to the next level with the "how," which often includes assumptions— the logical connecting of dots. "Three convenience store burglaries committed last week appear to have a similar modus operandi and were likely committed by the same assailants."

> *You can never determine whether a message is a microinequity or a microadvantage in a vacuum. It must be balanced against the way similar messages are delivered to others.*

Commentary crosses the line of facts and moves into the realm of opinion and conjecture. "There are several other such stores in that neighborhood but the stores targeted for these burglaries were all owned by families of Middle Eastern descent, suggesting these may have been hate crimes."

Editorialization takes the bold step into advocacy, telling us what we should do, feel, or believe about a news event. It is the reason for the Federal Communications Commission's provision of "Equal

Time" for broadcast news and "Op Ed" pages for print media. Giving the opposing political party equal time to present its views following the President's State of the Union speech is part of this attempt at balancing news bias.

News organizations don't oppose these practices. They recognize their unique power to influence (or is it shape) how people see the world. This is mostly done through the use of micromessaging. Even reportage, the purest, most neutral form of news delivery, has a wide spectrum of facts with which to paint multiple shades of a story. The decision of which facts to include, versus those subjectively omitted, can dramatically alter how someone walks away feeling about the story.

Most print and electronic news organizations use attitudinal or biased terms, such as *our*, when talking about the local sports team, or *beautiful* to describe a female crime victim. Reuters on the other hand, has carefully analyzed the powerful effect micromessages have on creating bias in reporting the news. This agency works extremely hard to present only the purest form of unbiased news delivery, with special attention on the subtle implications.

In the weeks following the events of September 11, American flags may have become the most ubiquitous window covering, second only to Levelor. On countless residential and commercial windows, store fronts, and in office building lobbies American flags were visible. Oh, yes, that Star-Spangled Banner waved "o'r" the land of the free, but not "o'r" the home of Reuters. Why? Because Reuters' company policy prohibits the display of national symbols in public areas.

When I first heard of this practice at a meeting in the company's Times Square offices, I was stunned, even irritated, at what seemed to be extreme insensitivity. How could displaying the flag in support of America, while lower Manhattan still smoldered, be a bad thing? Hrrumph! However, once fully explained, the policy became something I not only came to appreciate, but to advocate for a news agency.

If a guiding principle for presenting the news to the public is objectivity and an absence of bias, then words that incorporate the reporter's political, social, moral, or emotional frame of reference alter the purity of that objectivity. Even when referring to the hijackers of the four ill-fated airplanes, Reuters never used the word *terrorist*. Having personally been in Tower Number 2 of the World Trade Center that fateful morning, I do use that word—but I don't report the news to the public.

The word *terrorist* carries a clear indication of which side you're on as it relates to the action. A neutral alternative would be *bomber*. We've heard it said before, one person's terrorist is another's freedom fighter. Martin Luther King, Gandhi, Crispus Attucks, Nelson Mandela—even Jesus—were all troublemakers in the eyes of some. In news reporting, neutrality in reportage, analysis, and commentary should be king.

The journalist's goal must be to write the story in such a way that it could be broadcast in any country or culture and not spark an emotional reaction to its presentation. This is not political correctness. It is not for the purpose of appeasement. It is the way information should be presented to allow us to decide, without external influence, how we feel or whether we like or dislike the players or their actions.

Who Decides Attractiveness?

I first became aware of the power subtle shadings can have on shaping people's views when I traveled internationally. I read and listened to the accounts of world events through the eyes of local journalists. The variance, though accurate in fact, was dramatic.

Even the simple noun that was used to state who the story was about sometimes significantly altered the meaning. In a single day across two countries and seven news channels, I heard the terms, *the American government, the American people, the Bush administration, our allies, the American position, Washington,* and *the Yanks* used to indicate the subject in the reporting of the same news story. The choice of American reference indicated a position.

When I hear a broadcaster say, "A beautiful young college student was senselessly murdered last night," I am offended. Why does it matter how attractive she was? Is it sadder that an attractive girl was killed than an ugly one? And who defines attractiveness?

Tell me her age, not that she was young. I'll decide young from old for myself. And what are "senseless" murders anyway? Which are the murders that are sensible? The Reuters approach might present it as, "A 26-year-old woman was found dead in her apartment last night, the victim of two gunshot wounds. It is unknown whether there was a motive for the shooting." The impact of the bias created by the micromessages is a blind spot for both the journalist and Aunt Tillie as she watches the evening news.

Similar subtle choices find their way into the workplace and our personal lives. They seep through the cracks in the ways we define a colleague's role, describe details of a project, present a progress report, or write performance appraisals.

Expectations Become Reality

After checking into a New England hotel, I went straight for the restaurant. The bag of salty mini pretzels on my three-hour flight left me hungrier than had I eaten nothing at all. The restaurant's buffet style allowed me to get exactly what I wanted. It was winter and I had a craving for a cup of hot chocolate. I noticed the packets were a different brand than the last time I stayed at that same hotel, so I asked the waiter if they had anymore of those golden packets from a few weeks ago. The waiter paused in thought, looked upward, turned back toward me, and said, "I don't think we have anymore of those," and began walking away.

Now what the heck did that mean? Was that a no, or was he not sure? Call me easily amused, but that particular cup of hot chocolate was all I was looking forward to upon arrival. Pressing the issue, I called him back. "Are you *sure* you don't have anymore?" He shook his head saying, "Yea, I'm pretty sure. I haven't seen them in over a week now. They probably switched suppliers." He had just gone from thoughtful guessing to wild conjecture.

I had to ask the obvious next question. "You said you weren't sure. Is there anyone you could check with to be certain there aren't anymore in the back somewhere?" Seemingly wanting to be helpful, he picked up an intercom, and as he was dialing said, "Jake is in the stock room. I'll ask him." His question to Jake set off all my micromessaging alarms and sprinklers: "Jake, we don't have anymore of those gold color hot chocolate packets, do we?" Of course, Jake's reply was the predictable, "Uh, no, I don't think so." That slanted question ended all hope. Was that phone cord long enough to make a noose?

This guy was all that was standing between me and my much needed choco-fix and he had just posed a *make it go away* question. Reuters was about to get yet another opportunity for a new neutral headline. "The president of a New Jersey-based consulting firm attacked and severely assaulted a waiter at a Boston hotel yesterday. There was no apparent motive for the attack."

I felt an urgent need to do some counseling. This was no longer a hotel and he was no longer a waiter. I was no longer a thirsty hotel guest, but a consultant, and he was a pro-bono client. Yes, there were ulterior motives.

I blurted, "How could you ask the question that way and expect anything other than 'no' for an answer? The 'We don't have...do we?' made it not only easy for Jake to say no, but virtually told him to do so. Would you mind calling him back and trying this instead, 'Jake, I have a guest who would really like one of those gold packet hot chocolates. Would you please check and bring one to me when you find it?'"

The waiter was a bit reluctant, but after a ten-minute dissertation on micromessaging, he complied. Sure enough, Jake came strolling out a few minutes later with the stash. You must be wondering how good this hot chocolate could possibly be to go through such an effort. Write and I'll tell you the brand.

One leadership blind spot is the manner in which questions are asked. Questions often reveal what we want or expect the answer to be. Typically, the structure of a question falls into one of three forms: The assumptive no, the assumptive yes, and the neutral.

> *Questions often reveal what we want or expect the answer to be.*

You ask the question the way you want the answer to be. Sometimes questions aren't questions at all. Questions can be statements and statements can be questions. One such question (that isn't) is sweetly asked by my wife from time to time. It's usually Saturday night and I'll step out of the bedroom after spending an hour getting ready to meet friends for dinner. She'll gaze at me neutrally and ask, "Are you wearing that?"

Those four words may have grammatically ended with a question mark, but that was *no* question. Not even close. It was a statement that approached the level of a directive. "Change!" was the real message, and it didn't take too many years of living with her to figure it out. Rhetorical questions like this are either spoken to fill awkward silences, or they have an ulterior motive.

Carefully consider the micromessages within the questions you are asked, as well as those you are asking. Meetings and one-on-one sessions can waste precious time in a circular dance of questions chasing the wrong paths. Know what question is being asked and why the question is being asked and, if unclear, insert the trump question, "Why do you ask?" This is an effective technique that shines a search light on this blind spot.

At its core, the blind spot of leadership crops up when we say one thing, but telegraph something quite different. Our blindness is not linked to intelligence or level. We forget that intellect and performance are not inextricably linked. Some of the smartest people I have known are the worst perpetrators

> *Know what question is being asked and why the question is being asked and, if unclear, insert the trump question, "Why do you ask?"*

of microinequities: senior executives, entrepreneurs, authors, and academic luminaries. There may even be a direct correlation between higher intelligence and micromessage ineptness. I suppose if you have the credentials of academic superiority everything seen through your eyes must be the proper vision. It's a remarkable living irony that those responsible for providing guidance and knowledge often inflict the most damage. An unfortunate mantra: The higher their academic achievement, often the lower their micromessaging effectiveness.

Corporate senior executives are often oblivious to the effects of microinequities because they are rarely on the receiving end of these messages. Actually, what they experience the most are *microdeceptions*, more commonly known as pandering and brown-nosing. A senior executive never really knows if the nods of agreement and support are genuine or politically motivated. Even the employee can be confused. Do I think I agree with the boss because I've concluded that it's the best idea, or am I influenced by the source of the message?

> *Corporate senior executives are often oblivious to the effects of microinequities because they are rarely on the receiving end of these messages.*

To their credit, once executives are made aware of the effects of microinequities, this understanding becomes part of their DNA. When they grasp how the application of effective micromessaging changes how their employees work for them, it becomes absorbed into their being. In addition to having an interest in their own careers, most senior executives have a genuine ambition for organizational excellence.

Risky Role Playing

I was presenting an executive overview of our MicroInequities program to a Fortune 100 company considering a companywide rollout to their entire 60,000-person population. As I hoped—and expected—I was challenged by the CEO: "Steve, do you think people really notice these micromessages? Do they even see them and pick up on them?" he asked. In response, I did something I had never done before, and will probably never do quite the same way again.

There was one African-American man among the CEO's direct reports at this meeting and I asked him to stand next to me. I then reminded the CEO of all the social exchanges that preceded the meeting. I replicated some of the casual exchanges and introductions I'd engaged in while I was getting to know the members of the executive team right before we started.

I recreated precisely what I did when I approached the CFO. "Hi, Susan. Steve Young. Good to meet you." We chatted about a mutual friend, a CFO from another company. My interactions with the head of research were similar; I mentioned I'd read his article in a monthly business periodical and offered an opinion. The CEO also had no problems remembering my initial contact with him. "Jack, it's great to finally meet you," I played the chatter back for him. Jogging his memory, I reminded him that we had talked about a not-for-profit organization where he sits on the board, and how I'd praised some of the work it had been doing. I also reminded him that each encounter was about the same length and how I maintained a consistent friendly yet formal tone with all.

But then I asked the CEO if he remembered how I greeted Brad, the only other African-American in the room, who was now standing beside me. His face looked blank and puzzled, so I stepped back a bit, put some distance between Brad and me to reenact our greeting. Turning toward Brad, now about eight feet away, I began beaming a warm smile and strode toward him. I had ever so slight a sway and as we got nearer, I plunged my right hand toward his to shake it, then took hold of his forearm with my left hand, squeezing it as we continued to shake hands. "Hey, man. Steve Young. Really good to see you." No, we didn't do the fancy handshake.

I froze in position holding onto Brad's hand, my other hand clutching his forearm. I looked over to the CEO. It was clear he had seen and remembered it all. "Absolutely," he said, throwing his hands up. "I did notice it, but then the meeting started and it all sort of dissipated."

Being the smart and intuitive man that he is, he began making the connections. He said he now saw how the incident stretched well beyond the situation. He could imagine, he said, what it might be like if he were to walk into a meeting of black people where he was the only white person. He seemed to be thinking aloud as he said, "If they all greeted each other with that same warm affect but greeted me with an appropriate, but expressionless, 'Good morning. Glad you're here for the meeting.' I would definitely feel like an outsider." He was on a roll as he continued, "I can see how it would influence my performance. Everything I would do or say would be influenced by that greeting. They would be part of some warm, congenial club—I would notice it, feel left out, and, yes," he added, "it would certainly influence my performance and participation."

He took it to the next level, explaining how if they had done all of the so-called right things—politeness, courtesy, respect, it wouldn't have made a difference. In that short exchange, he clearly saw how doing the right thing plays a very small role in maximizing how others will participate and perform.

Suddenly there was a look of frustration. "Can you imagine what a complete idiot I'd look like if I attempted to talk to someone about this? Could you see me walking up to someone and saying, 'Excuse me, I want to talk about the way you said, hi, Jack, and how it was different from the way...'" He then understood how trying to articulate the experience of a microinequity would make him look overreactive and hypersensitive as well as how the positive or negative impact such micromessages could have on employee performance.

Several months after that session, the CEO spoke of how his staff began to feel comfortable calling him on any microinequities when he did them. They were comfortable saying, even to the senior executive, "Was that a microinequity?" He had even become comfortable hearing it, but, more importantly, he had begun to do something with the awareness. Knowing the potent impact micromessages have on relationships, commitment, and performance on the job, he began to alter how he conveyed his directives.

This CEO was an eyewitness to the impact this new addition to the lexicon has had in dissolving the barriers of power that have previously prevented open discussion. I like to think that everyone who has been exposed to this—and everyone who is reading this book—is building a common language to help define the messages we are constantly sending and receiving. This common language will, in turn, allow us to discuss openly what these messages are and how they affect us.

But as you will see in the next chapter, this new lexicon, in some ways, is much older than any words we currently use to communicate. Some scientists now believe the first written language dates back 9,000 years. Found in China, these early symbols, in the form of characters etched on tortoise shells, reveal much about our ability to codify visual language. It seems clear that humans have been greeting each other—sending micromessages of approval, connection, distance, hate, and cooperation—long before they carved symbols on shells after an evening of tortoise sushi.

CHAPTER 5

We're Wired That Way

We have all been there. You sit down in a quiet cozy restaurant, or recline your seat on a long transcontinental flight, just as a nearby baby starts to wail. Mom has tried to take a break by handing baby over to Dad, but it doesn't take long for the squealing and the reaching for Mom to begin. Dad tries in earnest to calm the baby, stiffly and awkwardly bouncing it to no avail. Dad isn't yet comfortable carrying his child, nor does he have any mastery of parenting at this stage, and his baby knows it; baby has gotten the message. Although the baby can't speak, she or he can read Dad's body language.

You may have heard how a group of Americans are now trying to toilet train their babies without diapers, by reading their child's needs through body language. The idea is that a parent, holding the child close, or just by watching the infant's movements, can predict when the child is getting ready to relieve himself or herself. By studying body language, the parents in this effort are becoming attuned to their child's physical needs. Contrary to what you might think, this isn't just a small cult of wacky parents with too much time on their hands.

The *New York Times* reported in an October 9, 2005 article[1] that diaper-free parenting is common in more than 75 countries,

---

[1] "A Fast Track to Toilet Training for Those at the Crawling Stage." *New York Times*, October 9, 2005.

including India, Greenland, China, and Kenya. I'm not sure why anyone would ever want to establish that sort of connection with their children, especially considering the consequences on days Mom or Dad are not at their most attentive, but it does illustrate how the most subtle of messages can reveal thoughts, feelings, and, well, pressing needs. It makes sense that babies can read our body language (and vice versa) quite well, even before they utter their first word. Parents can discern the difference between their baby's tired cry, hungry cry, angry cry, or cry of acute pain.

All of which is to say, the foundation of micromessaging is not new. The concept is at the root of human communication. No doubt our human ancestors became skilled at reading and interpreting subtlety and nuance in their communications thousands, or even hundreds of thousands, of years ago. While having only a series of grunts, roars, and the occasional chest-beating at their disposal, our prehistoric forebearers probably had little or no problem letting each other know how they were feeling after a long, wet, cold, day stuck in the cave. Our human forerunners cried tears of laughter at the misfortune of members of their group, long before our German counterparts got around to capturing this sensation with the term *schadenfreude*.

Research conducted at the Max Planck Institute for Evolutionary Anthropology in Leipzig, Germany suggests that our ability to speak developed quite recently on the human evolutionary ladder, which most scientists believe we've been climbing for about four million years. Something happened about 200,000 years ago, experts say, which gave human beings a leg up on other hominids; it was then that our ancestors began spreading around the globe. Coincidentally, around this time a new gene appeared that is linked to speech. According to the researchers at the Max Planck Institute, humans have the FOXP2 gene, while apes do not.

As spoken language evolved around 200,000 years ago, so did culture. Written language came later. In the West, Mesopotamian

Signs carved into 8,600-year-old tortoise shells found in China.
These may be the earliest known written words.

wedge-shaped images pounded into clay tables date as far back as 3500 B.C. More recently, turtle shells found in Neolithic graves in Henan province of China are thought to be from as early as 6500 B.C., more than 8,500 years ago.

The point is we were communicating through micromessages long before we communicated with words. Micromessages are a universally understood language, which we start interpreting and using virtually at birth. Virtually all humans are able to accurately read a baby's expression of contentment, fear, laughter, or anger. And when we respond, the baby understands and sends a return message that is, in essence, a confirmation.

> *Micromessages are a universally understood language, which we start interpreting and using virtually at birth.*

We sense that same safety or danger micromessages from colleagues and managers in the workplace. We're just not equipped
to talk about them.

Facial Expressions Give It Away

Facial expressions are universal. Dr. Paul Ekman advises Hollywood
on how to make monsters smile, and has spent most of his life studying how emotions register in the face. In fact, he has developed a system that charts which of the 43 muscles in the face are engaged in
each emotion. The system, called Facial Action Coding System, or
FACS, is now used around the world by neurologists, psychiatrists,
and psychologists. See the illustration on next page.

Ekman and his colleagues traveled to some of the farthest reaches
of the planet, including the mountains of Papua, New Guinea, where
there are no televisions, DVDs, or movies. There he discovered that
many facial expressions, including the smile, can be universally com-
prehended. Dr. Ekman filmed the expressions of this indigenous population and discovered their expressions were understood by
Westerners when he returned home. Ekman maintains that there are
seven basic emotions which can be read in facial signals: anger, sad-
ness, fear, surprise, disgust, contempt, and happiness.[2]

How long does it typically take for you to realize that you have
somehow angered your partner? How is it that you know your boss
is about to berate you for something a nanosecond before the
exchange begins?

A woman at one of my seminars a few years ago told a wonderful
story of how this had happened with one of her colleagues. The
woman said she had come into a meeting after having had a terrible

---

[2] Paul Ekman, W.V. Friesen, and J. C. Hager. *The Facial Action Coding System.* 2nd
ed. Salt Lake City, Research Nexus eBook, 2002.

It's not in the words. Subtle changes in facial expression have the power to dramatically alter the essence of a message. We don't see our own faces and as a result we are often unaware of the powerful micromessages these expressions convey. Each of these expressions carry a message beyond any words we might use to describe their differences in meaning.
Courtesy of Peter DaSilva Photography. All Rights Reserved.

argument with her husband and son. She was embarrassed about what had happened at home and didn't want anyone at work to know about the argument. About fifteen minutes into the meeting, a good friend leaned over and whispered, "Betty, what's wrong? Are you okay?"

Betty explained how she was absolutely stunned that her colleague could see through her mask and read the turmoil she was experiencing. She had made a proactive attempt *not* to transmit her feelings, but micromessages had betrayed her. Others in the room were oblivious to the incident, but because Betty's colleague knew her well, she was able to read the micromessage as though it were a thought bubble above her head.

Frankly, for those who know us well, each of us is a lot easier to read than we think. As a subordinate, you have intuitively read the silent or implicit messages from your boss about confidence, uncertainty, distance, and sincerity, for example. Working closely with others acquaints us with the micromessages we each use to communicate. But we're not the only creatures to use micromessaging.

> *Working closely with others acquaints us with the micromessages we each use to communicate.*

We can learn a lot about how humans communicate from other mammals. For some, you needn't go further than the pet at the end of the leash. Micromessages actually enable clear communication between you and your dog.

Micromessaging is the foundation of mammalian communication. Our ability to communicate in this manner transcends codified language. Some of the most prominent psychologists and linguists, including Noam Chomsky and Steven Pinker, agree that we were, in effect, having "conversations" with each other long before we could speak using language. Written language is a relatively new phenomenon, particularly when it is considered in the context of the two to four million years of *Homo sapiens'* existence.

Disclaimer: There are certainly many nonevolutionary beliefs about how we all arrived and how long we've been here. For this timeline, we are looking through the lens of evolution.

The average person's working vocabulary is about 20,000 words. With all those words to choose from, we still routinely screw things up. However you slice it, micromessaging established the platform for our communication roots and is still the method we inadvertently rely on for decoding the underlying message.

Birds do it, bees do it, and even little babies do it. Long before infants are able to speak, they are fully interactive through micromessages. You can look into a baby's face and clearly read curiosity, anger, disinterest, playfulness, fear, trust, and a host of thoughts and emotions. The baby, of course, reads and understands sounds and expressions as well. Without a single word, you can have an interactive exchange with someone possessing the verbal vocabulary of a goldfish.

Micromessaging is the foundation of mammalian communication. Our ability to communicate in this manner transcends codified language.

We were doing pretty well those hundreds of thousands of years ago, and then along came words. Although they certainly added more colors to the pallet, they also interfered with our use of red, green, and blue. Micromessages are the primary colors of communication and are the basis for how every "word color" is formed.

You Can Teach an Old Dog New Tricks

In the journal *Science*, German scientists reported that a dog had learned the meaning of nearly 200 words,[3] proving that dogs

---

[3] Paul Bloom, "Behavior: Can a Dog Learn a Word?" *Science*, Vol. 304, No. 5677, June 11, 2004, pp. 1682–1683.

understand human language. Researchers at the Max Plancke Institute reported that a Border collie named Rico could distinguish between 200 items—mostly toys—when told to fetch them. "Rico, wo ist der Banane?" his owners would ask; that is, "Rico, where is the banana?" And Rico would know to bring his toy shaped like a banana. The scientists set up experiments, telling Rico to put a specific toy in a box or to take it to a certain person. The objects were in a different room, confirming that the scientists were not signaling to Rico with their eyes or body language. Rico would leave the room, get the named toy, return, and do with it as instructed.

The scientists said the dog's ability to learn language supports the notion that some of the mechanisms underlying human language evolved "before humans were ready to talk." But as true as this may be, and as well as your dog understands you, you also understand your dog just as well. What enables you both to communicate, however, is not human language at all.

Before I owned a dog, when people told me they could sense their pet's feelings, thoughts, and emotions, and that their pet could detect their mood as well, I remember believing they were delusional. I even had people telling me they could tell when their dog was smiling. Well, I have a dog now and I know when he is smiling, frowning, confused, curious, frightened, guilty, and a host of other emotions. And it has nothing to do with the tail wagging. You could cut the tail off entirely and I would still know everything about my dog's state of mind.

So what is it that tells you your dog is smiling? Which physical attributes does he exhibit? You may feel that this is something you can easily describe, but when you put it to the test, you will find it almost impossible to relate exactly what that smile looks like using descriptive words to define what you see.

In the attempt to describe a smile, or happiness, people often use words like a "sparkle" or "brightness" in the dog's eyes. These are interpretive words that describe one's feelings, but not specific visual cues. We all understand what a sparkling eye is, but can't easily find words to describe what we physically observe. Audiences will often say that the eyes are big and wide open. "Okay, and where are these large eyes looking?" I ask. The response is always, "Right at me." Though this may sound reasonable, it is also true that when a dog's eyes are enlarged and looking directly at you, it is also precisely what a dog does just before it attacks.

If you own a dog, or indeed any other pet whose mood you claim to be able to accurately gauge, try to describe the physical attributes. You will find it difficult, to say the least. With careful thought you may describe the way the hair on the dog's back stands up, a position of the ears, movement of the head, accelerated breathing, or raised shoulders. These examples may bring you closer to the mark, but whatever it is you do see, you pick up on it instantly. You don't know exactly how you know, but you know. You're not aware of what you see, but you see it. As quickly and as often as you may do this, it's unlikely you've ever walked in the door, looked at the dog and reviewed some mental checklist, "Let's see, the eyes are sparkling. The hair on the back is slightly lifted. The head is bobbing. The shoulders are thrust forward and slightly elevated—great, he's happy!"

You can't easily describe the micromessages, but they tell you everything you need to know.

The bottom line is this: Without words, you immediately identify a host of emotions from your dog. You sense what he is thinking and feeling when he is with you. You can't easily describe the micromessages, but they tell you everything you need to know.

So, why all this talk about dogs? If you think you read your dog well, you read your colleagues even better. Just as quickly and clearly as you read that broad range of emotion from Fido or Fifi, you can also read the micromessages from your colleagues revealing what they think and feel about you, your ideas, and working with you in general.

While conducting a seminar in Arizona a few months ago, a woman quietly stepped out of the room and then returned waving a photograph announcing, "This is a picture of my dog smiling." Let me share with you Jody's "smiling" dog.

Jody's smiling dog.

The most memorable part of the discussion with Jody was her departing comment, "Now don't forget—this is only his half smile." At first glance, this picture seems like anything but a dog smiling. Your instinct probably leads you to see a growling, snarling, maybe even a smirking dog, but Jody's daily contact confirms the message. She interprets the dog's emotion, and then her interaction either validates the assumption or reveals the misinterpretation. Yes, a picture *is* worth a thousand words and, in this case, it is Jody's thousand hours of exposure that determines the accuracy.

I shared the photo with an animal trainer, who explained this is not unusual. There are breeds, dalmatians in particular, that, when you raise them as puppies, holding and cuddling them, they begin to interpret the micromessages associated with human actions and expressions of happiness and pleasure. Some dogs will even attempt to replicate a human smile. Yes, in some cases, it ends up looking like this. But this is all Jody's dog is doing.

As a child, I was always amazed at how television took this human to dog communication to the next level. Midway through the program, Lassie would have cause to sprint home and deliver her well-rehearsed lines to Timmy's mother. There would be ten seconds or so of passionate barking and mother would say, "What's that, Lassie? Timmy fell down the mine shaft? You think he may have fractured his femur? You brought him some water and a tourniquet before you left? Good girl! I'll get the doc and we'll follow you."

There are some limits of course, but at age ten, it seemed perfectly plausible. After all, Timmy and Lassie were best friends, just like Barry and I. Barry was deaf and I knew absolutely nothing about sign language. It didn't matter. I understood Barry's eyes, gestures, and facial expressions better than the unintelligible mumbling from some of the other kids. Barry and I never thought that we weren't talking simply because we weren't using words. With Barry, though it came easily; I was conscious of reading all of his

subtle expressions. Strange, but I foolishly never thought of applying those skills to consciously read my first boss, Neil.

Neil believed he was the world's greatest manager. He so
strongly held that opinion that he was able to convince several of
us to buy in. Oblivious to the micromessages, I was lulled into an
acceptance of his mediocrity. His performance as a leader was
inconsistent among the team members, with several of us getting
the short end of the stick and thinking it was just a natural pick of
the draw.

Take a tip from my relationship with Barry: Read your relationship with your manager through a new dimension by examining
the differences in the messages you receive and those being sent to
others using the same words. Monitor the feedback you get and, if
it sounds similar to what others are receiving, look more closely to
determine whether yours is saying half empty while others are
being told half full. Are your assignments difficult because the goals
are unattainable, or are they challenging but within your grasp? As
the boss, monitoring how you manage these and other elements
builds your effectiveness as a leader.

We read micromessages well when we're young, but somehow
we seem to lose the ability as we get older. As a young boy I would
always buy my Dad a tie for Father's Day. I would also buy him a
tie for his birthday. Yes, Christmas too. As a boy, I wasn't terribly
creative in the gift department. My gift always came in the same,
long thin-shaped box. Heaven knows why I even wrapped it. He
would smile, look stumped, open the "mystery" package, and fondle
the tie with great appreciation.

No one else could tell but within five seconds I knew exactly
how many times we would see it around his neck over the next six
months. If I caught a little glint in his eye, I knew I would see the
new neckwear once a week. But if there was a twist of the nose, I
recognized it would likely become middle drawer artwork. Funny
thing was, I never thought about what was happening. I just knew

what I needed to know. I'm sure you were able to do the same sort of thing with a parent or close loved one. Many of you certainly read similar messages from a parent at an early age. It may have been the way your name was called, or which name they chose to call you. It doesn't take a tremendous amount of effort to heat up that skill again and apply it to the many relationships in the workplace.

It's fascinating how children learn a language. I was very young when I learned how to read Dad and Barry's micromessages, but all of us learn these subtleties and their use in common language. We learn about the importance of noun order and its sensitivity in the structure of a sentence. No one needs to explain to a small child that when two nouns are placed together the first always modifies the second. For instance, *boat house* is quite different from *houseboat* and you wouldn't want to confuse *house cat* with *cat house*. The fundamentals of these nuances can be acquired with some work, when learning a second language as an adult, but children pick them up instinctively. Sometimes our instinct subconsciously reveals our hidden thoughts when dealing with colleagues. The placement and order of words can expose, in ways that we may not want to reveal, how we feel about others. Choose your words and their sequence carefully.

> *The placement and order of words can expose, in ways that we may not want to reveal, how we feel about others. Choose your words and their sequence carefully.*

Instant Micromessaging

Instant messaging has become a central part of the way we communicate electronically. In the workplace, a different sort of "instant message" reaches well beyond the dimensions of the computer screen and can be quicker, clearer, and without that annoying "ping" announcing a new message.

Each of us has attended meeting after meeting with a team member we like and admire. Without ever saying a word, she gets the message you unconsciously but repeatedly send: "Pat, you are so smart. You always cut through all the garbage and get right to the heart of the issue every time. People look up to you. You're a role model."

In that same meeting, to someone else on the team you may have sent very different messages. Still void of a single word, he hears: "You really are a jerk. How did you get this job in the first place anyway? This team would be so much better off without you."

If the sender of the message has the "stripes" of power or authority, the message will have a powerful effect on participation and performance at meetings. Neither party will likely make the connection between those micromessages and the recipient's performance. But, these messages will affect participation, the expression of new ideas, the willingness to challenge the boss and even others in the room. Your action when these messages are observed become the accelerator of leadership effectiveness.

Birds do it, bees do it, and you did it instinctively in childhood. If you are not constantly observing micromessages in all the modes you communicate, your skills may need revamping. Before I go on to discuss how we continually communicate with and interpret this unspoken language with our colleagues, let me first demonstrate another example of how micromessages go deeper than written or spoken language. They are a part of the DNA, the innate underlying understanding we have with each other simply because we are all human beings.

CHAPTER 6

I Didn't Say She Stole the Book

S ubtle inflections can alter the core meaning of a message. Sometimes just putting the emphasis on a different word transforms the whole meaning of a statement. You just have to listen carefully to discover how a small change can transform everything about what is *really* being conveyed. The next segment will make this observation very clear. You will probably laugh out loud in the middle of it, but a number of light bulbs will also go on.

You're now going to read a seven-word sentence six times aloud. (Reading these sentences silently won't give the full measure of the effect.) Each time, place the emphasis on a different word. The words themselves will not change. The only change will be what you make the listener focus on. Here's your sentence:

I didn't say she stole the book.

Start by reading the sentence with the emphasis on, "I." *I* didn't say she stole the book. The meaning: It wasn't I who said it. Someone else made the remark, so leave me out of it!

Now put the stress on, "didn't." I *didn't* say she stole the book. The meaning: A statement of denial. I never made that remark.

Here's my personal favorite: Put the emphasis on "say." I didn't *say* she stole the book. As you do, pause briefly just before the word say then slightly raise your palms while saying the word. The message: I damn well know she did it, but I kept my mouth shut.

In the next iteration, the focus on the word *she* makes it clear that the listener only misunderstood who you were accusing. I didn't say *she* stole the book. It's clear to everyone the book was stolen, just not by her.

Now, as you emphasize the word "stole," bring your two hands to your chest level and point your palms outward. I didn't say she *stole* the book. She definitely has the book, but may have inappropriate possession with no malicious intent. Maybe she was just borrowing it and forgot to return it.

Actually, this one is my favorite. As you emphasize the word *book*, open your eyes a bit wider. I didn't say she stole the *book*. This version of the sentence suggests ambiguity as to what was stolen. There's certainly no question she's a thief; the only question is, "What exactly did she walk off with?"

In the world of emotion, words rarely tell the whole story. Without changing a single word of the sentence, and only moving the emphasis, the sentence had six very different meanings. We do this sort of thing routinely as a part of our daily communication in the workplace. The emphasis on the words we use with a particular person are often influenced by our personal feelings. We never stop to carefully analyze the gestures and movements associated with specific words, but the messages are nevertheless sent, and somehow subconsciously understood, by the receiver. Words and micromessages are ongoing competitors, but when the topics involve elements that drive work relationships, micromessages always score the knockout punch.

> Words and micromessages are ongoing competitors, but when the topics involve elements that drive work relationships, micromessages always score the knockout punch.

All our lives, we have been told that words are very important. The size of one's vocabulary is often a sign of intelligence and education. A solid grasp of grammar and word usage is essential for acceptance in most business communities. Industries make millions selling courses designed to improve vocabulary and writing composition skills. Yes, words are important, but when you compare words to what's wrapped around them in the delivery, they pale in comparison. The impact and influence of the unspoken messages being sent is even stronger than the words.

Influential Inflections

Think about how verbal inflections can taint how a manager asks for suggestions during a staff meeting. Say, someone on the team offers an idea. The manager listens politely and, when the team member concludes, the manager responds with the typical, "Great." Then she looks around the table and adds, "Any other ideas?" The interpretation of *great* can range from being truly impressed to a transition for moving on.

> *Yes, words are important, but when you compare words to what's wrapped around them in the delivery, they pale in comparison.*

More importantly, think about the word *other*, which can imply *alternate* or *better*. All too often *other* really means better, but those at the table tend to lean toward the literal meaning—alternate. In your own meetings, begin listening for the frequency of *other* when ideas are put up for consideration. If the word isn't preceded with commentary about the idea's value, such as "Excellent suggestion. Let's build on that...," you can bet it's probably a request for something better.

Turn the lens around. Instead of trolling for the behaviors in a meeting, plant a mental alarm that will ring whenever you use the term *other* or any other key micromessaging terms. You may be surprised to observe how team members will offer a larger volume of contributions, as well as more "out of the box" ideas. Taking the time to verbalize your reaction and assessment of team members' contributions can move the thinking in new directions.

The inflection we use and the ways in which it alters the core meaning in sentences show themselves in all our relationships. My son, for example, had done something that was really quite devilish, but it was adorable. I grabbed his head, pulled him to my chest, rubbed my knuckles in his hair, and said, "You are such a *monster*." Although my words said one thing, clearly my message said, "I adore you." Later the same day, in response to something my wife did, I looked at her, put my hands on my hips, slowly closed then opened my eyes and said, "That was *brilliant!*" If words are so powerful, how could the word monster mean, "I adore you" and *brilliant* mean, "You're an idiot." It is entirely in the micromessaging that we come to understand what is *really* being said.

You can see how this quickly translates to the work environment. You walk into your manager's office and she says, "Yes, what can I do for you?" But she does not look up; in fact, she continues to work on responding to her e-mails. You start speaking but occasionally pause, wondering if what you're saying is getting through. Of course, when the awkwardness of your protracted pause becomes uncomfortably noticeable, she turns, gives a "keep going" gesture and returns to the screen. You decide to be bold and ask if you should come back another time. She stops for a moment and offers a brief comment on the volume of work she has and the need for multitasking.

You feel a little foolish for not being more flexible, but something in your gut tells you you're not in the "inner circle." If more multitasking is such an important and acceptable business process, why does she always stop, turn, and focus when her boss stops by to chat?

If multitasking is such a good thing, why isn't it good for all levels? In fact, there may be team members who receive the same level of focus and attention your manager gives to her boss when they walk in with questions. The treatment you've just received is a microinequity, which is likely to neg-atively impact your productivity and work attitude.

The sender of a micromessage that includes a microinequity is often unaware that his or her prejudice against an individual is apparent.

But how would that change if your boss looked up, smiled with her eyes, and asked you to sit down, using your name. And then asked what she could do for you? Dr. Mary Rowe learned from her research on microinequities, which we discussed in previous chapters, that the sender of a micromessage that includes a microinequity is often unaware that his or her prejudice against an individual is apparent. "What can I do for you?" coming from your manager seems harmless enough, but the way in which the question is delivered can do the damage of a body blow.

Micromessages, Macroimpact

A dancer told me a story that captures the essence of how a person in power can quickly undermine performance. She was studying for the summer with one of America's greatest modern dancers, Martha Graham, who was quite senior in years at that point. The woman was still at the start of her own professional training, and when Miss Graham, famous for her sternness and her impatience, attended the elementary class, the woman became quite nervous. Simple steps that she could normally execute became difficult before Martha Graham's critical eye. After the woman danced past the great legend, Miss Graham shouted at her, "That's abysmal!" This completely threw the young dancer off and, of course, made it impossible for her to focus for the rest of class—or learn anything else that day.

If you, as a manager, rush to judge, sending microinequities of impulse and emotion that go beyond offering constructive commentary, your micromessages can have a greater impact than you may have intended. Besides, the quick assessment is often not an accurate reflection of a worker's or performer's true ability. How do you know if they have the ability to get "the steps" right? In the end, the person may not work out, but until he or she is given the same encouragement as someone whom you trust and feel confident about, you cannot accurately judge whether or not the person has the ability to perform the job well.

> *Micromessages are the keys that unlock—or shut down—potential.*

Dr. Rowe points out that microinequities, while seemingly small, are not trivial in their impact. Not only do they cheat someone who may have something to contribute, but they also may cheat an organization of the best parts of an employee's talent. Micromessages are the keys that unlock—or shut down—potential.

Out of the Mouths of Babes

My own children have helped me see that I'm not immune to sending microinequities. My daughter and I were discussing a friend of hers, whom I admit I'm not terribly fond of. When I made some comments that were actually quite harsh about her friend, my daughter looked at me with daggers and said, "Dad, that was obnoxious. I can't believe you said that about her. If she heard that she would be devastated. I'm personally insulted by that. You should apologize!"

I considered her comments and thought, "Maybe it was a little harsh, but I really don't like her." I looked at my daughter and, waving my hands in the middle of my chest, breathed a deep sigh and, said, "Fine, Alex! If you were offended by that, then I'm sorry. Okay?"

She looked at me, in a way that suggested I looked quite foolish, sort of in the way you might snicker if the person speaking to you had spinach stuck to their teeth. She put her hands on her hips, shook her head, and said. "Did you hear all those microinequities?" (That question from my daughter was reminiscent of Dr. Frankenstein's experience. I've given this "creature" the power and now it has predictably turned on me and I am, somehow, going to still enjoy it all happening.)

My response, as always: "Run it down for me, Alex." She began by saying she would save the best for last, and then began her lecture. "First of all, who, if they were sincere and genuine about an apology, would ever start it off with a big sigh and the word 'Fine.' And what's with all that movement of your hands? And don't let me leave out the expression on your face. Your facial muscles are telling me everything about what you're really thinking."

She went on. "Who would ever end a real apology with the word 'Okay'? That tells me you're just saying it to get me off your back, and not because you really mean what you're saying."

She had me in the corner.

"Oh, yea, and the best part...," she continued, ready to deal the final blow, "was that word in the middle of your so-called apology."

Like a moth to the flame, I foolishly asked, "What word?"

"If," she informed me.

"So what's the big deal with that?" I asked.

"Dad, no one ever uses the word 'if' in an apology when they genuinely mean it."

I opened my mouth, about to defend myself, but what could I say? She was right. She finished it off with, "If you were at one of those big conference tables in the office and knocked over someone's cup of coffee, would you ever turn and say, 'If that caused you a problem, I'm sorry?' Since when have real apologies come with conditions attached?" She couldn't resist capping the opportunity with a summary lesson. "If you knocked over that cup of coffee, your eyes, facial expression, tone, inflection, your hands, head, the speed of your sentence, all would say, 'Oh, I'm so sorry.' And they would know that you meant it. In this case, I know you didn't." Of course, she was right.

Certainly everyone reading this book has received that sort of apology. And, don't deny it; you've all given apologies like that as well. You have probably never focused on the underlying meaning of what the words are really saying.

We play a version of the Emperor's New Clothes. We convince ourselves that everything is fine because we said the right words and did all the right things. The person issuing the apology thinks, "I said I was sorry. It's done." Even the person receiving the apology says, "He apologized. What else is there?" But the person receiving the apology hears the apology on the same level it was given. The subtle message, the one felt at our core, is very different and often missed. We can't talk about it because we would be perceived as being overly sensitive because, after all, the right words were said.

In my daughter's case, I remained unkindly disposed toward her friend. But I did feel obligated to comply with something I was expected to do, so I offered the apology. With her skill around micromessaging, my daughter was able to take this to a far more effective level. We actually discussed my feelings about the friend and although we didn't come to agreement, we both walked away with a clear understanding about where we each stood on the issue.

Out of the Mouth of Bosses

Apologies are one of the most common ways we delude ourselves into believing we have sent the right message when, in fact, its interpretation can often be quite different. In the case of apologies, the sender and the receiver can be equally unaware of the true message being sent.

The ways we structure apologies provide an excellent platform to analyze how micromessages reveal the underlying hidden meaning of our message.

Let's take a look at the nature of conditional words as we analyze two case studies that illustrate how these messages can either be obligatory and off-putting, or interpreted as genuine and remorseful.

Our first example involves Michael Nifong, the former prosecutor of the highly publicized Duke University Lacrosse players rape case.

Nifong was up for re-election and running behind in the polls. There was great pressure from the community to secure a conviction of the three students who were accused in the rape of the young women hired to entertain a group of fraternity brothers at their on-campus frat house.

When it became clear, early on, that there was insufficient evidence to prosecute the students, Michael pushed the prosecution, nonetheless. Nifong feared that releasing the three suspects would ensure a loss in his re-election bid and even as more and more evidence surfaced supporting the students' innocence, Michael continued the case. His actions appeased the emotions of the community and he was re-elected.

When it became evident that his actions were a miscarriage of justice, the State of North Carolina intervened, removed Nifong from office, and the three students were immediately released by the Court.

As the clear facts of their innocence lay before him, Michael Nifong decided to issue the following public apology:

> *To the extent that I made judgments that ultimately proved to be incorrect, I apologize to the three students who were wrongly accused.*

It doesn't take expert analysis to recognize the deflection within Nifong's apology. Clearly this statement would be interpreted as obligatory and not heartfelt.

Let's do a careful analysis to uncover the structural components that reveal the nature of his choice of words that caused this interpretation.

Revealing the Nature of Conditional Words

We cannot be effective at changing the behavior of others when we merely express our emotions and reactions alone. A very natural reaction to the things that cause us to judge a message is to express what we have heard using words of emotion.

Someone reacting to Michael Nifong's apology might say the apology felt cold, insincere, indifferent, or obligatory but those are simply expressions of emotions and conclusions. Clearly, no one can "DO" an *insincere* or an *obligatory*. They are not tangible or manageable actions that can drive change.

When someone changes their behavior solely based on someone's feelings, the change in behavior tends to merely accommodate or make the other person feel better—not necessarily because they genuinely understand the advantage of doing it differently. Their changed behavior is based on accommodation, not logic and reason.

It's critical that we shift our focus away from simple feelings and conclusions, and instead create a new lens that identifies the specific actions that can be outlined to drive change.

Let's look back at Michael Nifong's apology and analyze the tangible elements that would cause one to reach a negative conclusion.

Nifong begins his apology with, "*To the extent that...*"

Let's stop right there. Any apology that begins with a conditional phrase conveys, right out of the gate, that the rest of the apology is not likely to be remorseful.

He then follows with, "*... that ultimately proved...*"

What does "ultimately" imply here? It suggests that his actions weren't always wrong, or, *I was right in the first place*!

He continues with, "*...ultimately proved to be incorrect.*"

It's quite telling when people choose to use the word *incorrect* instead of *wrong*. After all, doesn't it feel so much better to be *incorrect* than wrong? *Incorrect* even has the word *correct* in it!

He ends the apology with "*I apologize to the three students who were wrongly accused.*"

It's likely that Michael Nifong will believe in his mind, and in his heart, that he sincerely apologized to the three students. He will remember the second half of his apology:

I apologize to the three students who were wrongly accused.

But it's the micromessages in the first half of his statements that tell us the true nature of his message.

Even the second half of the apology reveals interesting information about his feelings of remorse.

Let's take a moment and look at just this segment alone and see if you can identify any revealing micromessages.

...I apologize to the three students who were wrongly accused.

Did you notice that he only apologized to the three students? Even if you knew nothing about this case, one could easily conclude that many other people were harmed by his mishandling of the case. The students' families, the University, its reputation, the town, the Lacrosse team, and of course, the high costs to the taxpayers for this unnecessary prosecution were certainly injured parties, as well.

Next, you'll notice he depersonalized the students by not using their names. There were only three of them! It wouldn't have extended the apology very much to include their names. Had he used their names, the apology would likely have seemed far less hollow.

Also, this segment of the apology was in the passive voice:

...who were wrongly accused versus *who I wrongly accused.*

Let's look at his last word in the apology: *accused.*

Although accurate, it doesn't acknowledge the more damaging issue. The students were not just accused, they were prosecuted!

Here's another interesting point about the word *accused.* Nifong was a District Attorney. The roles in our judicial system are clearly defined; District Attorneys don't accuse—they charge and prosecute. Grand Juries indict and the police arrest. So, who does the accusing?—The victim!

What Michael subtly did with his micromessaging was to blame the victim. This is probably why he chose to use the expression *wrongly accused* (the victim's actions) versus incorrect judgment which are his actions.

Nifong probably spent a fair amount of time crafting his apology. Yet, this is what he came up with—an apology filled with micromessages that deflect accountability or remorse.

Let's now take a look at a second example that represents the other side of the coin and shows how the micromessages can transform impact and effectiveness.

Shirley Sherrod, an African American woman, was a senior official at the U.S. Department of Agriculture. She was forced to resign after a recorded segment of a speech that she had given was lifted and placed on a popular political blog. It's important to mention that Ms. Sherrod's father had been killed by a white supremacist group many years in the past, leaving her with very strong feelings of racial animosity.

During her speech to the NAACP, she made the following statement:

A white farmer approached me asking for help with saving his farm, since I worked at the Agriculture department. And, I thought to myself, "He's a white guy. He's probably like those others." So, I didn't give him the full force of what I could do. I directed him to a white lawyer so that someone of his own kind would take care of him.

In all ways possible, all hell broke loose. That excerpt was clearly interpreted as intentionally choosing not to assist the farmer because he was a white man. The press had a field day and the White House erupted. How embarrassing that a senior government official would make such a terribly racist remark in front of a public audience. Shirley was called on the carpet to explain her behavior to her superiors.

She told them the statement was taken out of context and that they needed to consider the *entire* speech. The government officials made it clear that, in their minds, it didn't really matter what else she might have said. Having made that racist remark was grounds to demand her resignation. Immediately after her meeting with government officials, Shirley resigned.

Several days later the Agriculture department received a copy of the entire speech. In it, Shirley's next words transformed what her true message was:

> *...and then I thought to myself, how foolish that is. Why should I ever blame someone because they look like someone that did something wrong to me or my family? I went right back to the farmer, told him what I had done. I apologized and then personally took him through the process to help him; and in fact, he and his wife and I are still close, personal friends.*

Upon learning the full context of her speech, the Agriculture department didn't just need to apologize, they genuinely wanted to apologize.

It was Tom Vilsack, the U.S. Secretary of the Agriculture, who issued the apology. Here is what he said:

> *One of the lessons I learned is that these types of decisions require time. I didn't take the time. I should have.*
>
> *I indicated to Shirley my personal regret and my responsibility for the fact that she received multiple phone calls. That's, again, a problem that I could have corrected if I had done this job properly.*
>
> *I made a very hasty decision which I deeply regret. I could have done and should have done a better job.*
>
> *Tom Vilsack,*
> *U.S. Secretary of Agriculture*

Let's examine the micromessages that place Tom Vilsack's apology in a different hemisphere of impact from Michael Nifong's approach in the previous apology we explored.

Take a moment and read Tom Vilsack's apology again. See if you can identify some of the micromessages that make it more effective.

When analyzing this case in my public seminars, one of the first observations people make is that Vilsack is clearly taking accountability and responsibility. But words such as accountability and responsibility fall within the realm of feelings and emotions and are ill-defined.

One mission of this book is to build the skills that go beyond merely identifying feelings and conclusions.

People have little impact in changing the behaviors of others by expressing how the behavior made them feel. We must develop a new lens that identifies the indisputable, tangible elements that caused the feelings to be reached.

It is far more critical to be able to put your finger on the tangible components that are the causes of the feelings.

So, looking through this new lens, what word in Vilsack's apology demonstrates the conveyance of accountability?

Clearly, it is the simple word, "I." There are actually nine of them in this apology.

Too often apologies are given in the third person. Phrases such as "It's unfortunate that you felt that way," "Mistakes were made," "It shouldn't have happened..."

In the beginning of the apology, Vilsack uses the expression "lessons I learned." This is a powerful expression. It becomes indisputably clear that the sender of the message is remorseful and, because he or she has acknowledged learning something, he or she is unlikely to commit the act again.

Let's look at the impact this can have in influencing a recipient's reaction to an apology.

A common apology might be the following:

I'm really sorry about what I did; it was a mistake and it shouldn't have happened; I apologize.

Compare that to a different approach using the expression, *lessons learned:*

I'm sorry about what I did and I have to say I really learned something from this. The next time I see your, or anyone's name in a document, I should always go to that person before drawing any conclusions or taking any actions. I won't do that again. I'm sorry.

It goes without saying that the latter approach would be far more effective.

If someone had given me that first apology, I would likely respond by saying thank you, but might then turn to a friend and say, "That guy is a real jerk."

On the other hand, had I received the second version, there would be little chance that I would utter any disparaging remarks.

Lessons learned can have a profound effect on how you are embraced, post-apology.

Vilsack is very clear and direct about his most critical error:

I didn't take the time. I should have.

Effective apologies always make clear what was done and what should have been done differently.

His second paragraph makes it clear that he has already spoken with Ms. Sherrod and expressed to her his personal regret. He continues by addressing what she publicly stated was one of the most disruptive and distressing aspects of the entire experience—the phone calls.

An important message here is that no matter how insignificant something may seem to be, or may actually be, it is necessary to address it.

Remember those nine "I"s? Let's look at how powerful they are by removing them. Take a look at what the apology would sound like if we were to remove the "I"s and "my"s alone:

One of the lessons learned is that these types of decisions require time. Enough time wasn't taken and there should have been. It's been made clear to Shirley how regrettable it was that she received multiple phone calls. That's, again, a problem that could have been corrected if things had been done properly. A very hasty decision was made which is deeply regrettable. A better job could have been and should have been done.

The edited version will otherwise be verbatim, except to make it grammatically correct. That one change to Vilsack's apology transformed how most people interpret his remorsefulness.

If you were to read one or the other version of these apologies in the news, you would probably not stop to count the "I"s or notice that they were missing. You would, however, have a very different emotional reaction when reading it.

When we look at the workplace, it is essential that leaders come to terms with how these subtle methods of delivering our messages, micromessages, have a similar effect on the loyalty, motivation, and inspiration of those with whom they work and influence.

In the workplace, we frequently feel obligated to make statements we don't truly believe, but the micromessages reveal our core feelings. We send thousands of messages like these, which allow us to believe we are doing all the right things. The underlying micromessages send a nearly invisible signal that, almost like a dog whistle, can't be heard. Whether in Europe, Asia, Latin America, the United

States, or even in the comfort of our own homes, micromessages drive how we react and reveal the essence of what is being said. I remember many years ago a colleague saying that he had apologized a thousand times but rarely had he been remorseful.

CHAPTER 7

It's Here, There, and Everywhere

Cross-Cultural Microinequities

A senior banking executive I know was on temporary assignment in Hong Kong, leading a team of local analysts. During the first two weeks on the job, he would respond to information he was wary of the same way he did in New York. "Come on," he would say, cocking his head and furrowing his brow. "Are you sure?" he would ask, with a mildly sarcastic tone. What he didn't know was that he was quickly and effectively alienating every staff member he worked with. What he perceived as insignificant neutral messages became powerful microinequities when received through the filters of the local culture. In New York, such questions were part of office banter, but in Hong Kong, they suggested a lack of trust. Unbeknown to him, he was systematically insulting every member of his team.

Gradually, the staff became less responsive, although no one ever said a word directly. Just as questioning a report was taboo in Hong Kong, so was informing a colleague that he or she was screwing up or making other employees annoyed. This executive was left to keep repeating his mistakes and digging a deeper hole for himself. He recognized that his team was giving him less than 100 percent, and that the information he received seemed to be less than complete, but he had no idea why. His inability to read his team's micromessages had created a blind spot in his management of the team.

Fortunately, he learned what was going on while back in New York at a meeting. Another executive who had spent two years in Hong Kong told him what he heard through the grapevine. Armed with this new information, the executive quickly learned how to be more effective.

I later heard that, although it took a few months, his one-on-one mea culpas turned things around. Through the experience, his team reshaped their filters in the ways they judged what otherwise would be perceived as microinequities.

Here's another example, which deals with a cross-cultural business discussion in Tokyo. A colleague told me how he'd asked someone there to pull together some data for a meeting the following morning. The subordinate responded with a head nod and a sucking-air-through-the-teeth sound. The visiting American manager thought that meant, "Wow! That'll take a lot of work but you're the boss. No problem!" However, the real message being sent was, "Yes, I understand, but, sorry boss. That's just not at all possible."

You can imagine how that played out the following morning, when the boss had made promises and felt let down. Likewise, the employee felt frustrated because his boss hadn't accurately understood him, which caused embarrassment for the visiting manager. Lack of familiarity with local culture and micromessages makes it difficult for employees at all levels to function effectively.

Each business operation is colored by the cultural context in which it operates. The same pressure from the top that might improve individual worker performance in Singapore, might have the opposite effect in Ireland. Holding your body

> *Each business operation is colored by the cultural context in which it operates.*

Micromessages are universal in application. All cultures have their unique forms of sending and receiving these messages. But when you use your own filters, you run the risk of making faulty conclusions and unintentionally damaging your effectiveness in communities outside your own. You cannot interpret another culture through your own cultural lens. You must first become aware of both the regional and corporate culture through which your message is being received. The culture you are immersed in, not necessarily your own, should act as the barometer for shaping the micromessages you send and how you read the ones that you receive.

erect and puffing out the chest might be necessary for a boss to command respect in a Latin American culture, but the same stance could be read as bullying or arrogance in Ireland. Conversely, a slightly shy, round-shouldered American executive who always looks down might be judged an unworthy opponent, and therefore ineffective, in more macho cultures.

Observations of workplace culture in Ireland reveal that sending micromessages communicating the desire to collaborate with colleagues as equals is the key to getting a team to work together for a common purpose. At the same time, flagrant exhibitions of title or authority often are met with heated resistance—a surefire path to getting little done. Some visiting managers have learned the hard way that if you try to forcefully dictate to one of your peers, or even a subordinate, what, when, and how you want a directive to be carried out, it's likely you'll end up being the one carried out! On the other hand, visiting managers have been surprised at the devoted hard work they've elicited from an Irish team after they take the time to solicit opinions, encourage input, and make others feel they are part of the decision-making process.

The tradition of minimal command and control in the workplace remains part of a cultural norm that engages performance and national behavior in Ireland. Even those born into today's independent state adopt an Irish identity that puts each worker in control of what, when, and how he or she works for you.

In Hong Kong, the sort of tough truths that the Irish are willing to listen to when treated as equals, can prove ultimately disastrous in the workplace. Whereas in the United States it is quite common for a manager to give an employee direct, matter-of-fact feedback, it can be disastrous in some cultures. Try saying, "Your report has a massive number of mistakes. I can't believe you even submitted this to me," to an employee in Hong Kong and the relationship will likely be irreparably damaged. Furthermore, criticize the staffer in the presence of other colleagues, and chances are your relationship is over.

In Hong Kong, as in Tokyo, the more effective approach to voicing your displeasure with a project would be to say, "Would you please review the document once again and look for any opportunities to make revisions. You might pay particular attention to pages 4 and 6." The right message is conveyed, without causing the worker to lose face or feel insulted.

A colleague of mine, a marketing executive for a drug company, told me about going to a meeting in Japan where he was promoting a product he hoped the Japanese company would want to bring to market there. As the participants gathered in the conference room, he asked if everyone would please take a seat and got right down to the business of his presentation. He had only personally spoken with three of the ten attendees before that point. He was confident things were going well since he had never seen such vigorous head nodding before. By the end of his presentation, he was sure the adoption of the product was a shoe-in. So he was stunned to discover that he had not even gotten to square one.

He learned the hard way that no decisions are made by a group in the business climate in which he was operating. Besides, he left several questions unanswered, largely because they were not asked—because they wouldn't normally be asked in a group setting.

The most effective way to uncover the real issues and drive a decision would have been to meet each and every person on the team, one-on-one. During the private meetings, he would say exactly the same thing he'd said in the presentation. However, in a more intimate setting, the businessmen would have felt more comfortable asking questions.

The nods, the smiles, all the micromessages that in an American conference room would be taken for approval, in Japan only implied simple comprehension—little more than, "I hear you."

Intranational Microinequities

Cross-cultural micromessages also get sent and misinterpreted within a country. Microinequities are a part of intranational communications breakdowns, particularly when it comes to communications between the cosmopolitan regions of a country and its provinces. For example, Northern Italians hailing from Florence and Milan have a great deal of trouble treating their fellow country folk with the same respect they give one another. They think of the Southern Italians as peasants or farmers. When they come together in the workplace, the messages of hierarchy are subtle, but clear.

Similarly, the provincial French are quite used to thinking that their Parisian cousins are from another country entirely, since so steeply do some well-heeled Parisians look down their noses at the "provincials."

The Wrong Micromessage

While visiting Paris on business, I recently committed my own faux pas and was consequently insulted by a maître d' at one of the city's finer restaurants—and I deserved it! We had finished our meeting at noon and the senior business manager offered to take me to lunch at a traditional French restaurant. Although I had planned to stroll the Champs Élysées for a little shopping before heading to the airport, I decided this was a much better opportunity. Thinking I might be able to squeeze in both, as we stepped into the foyer, I asked my colleague to ask the maître d' if we could get out within an hour. My friend had a bit of an odd expression that seemed to silently say, "Okay, you're the guest." I watched as my request was delivered in French and an interesting expression formed on the maître d's face as he flashed his eyes in my direction. His response was fluent even to someone who doesn't speak the language.

My colleague delivered the answer, "Tell your friend that if he just wants to gobble down some food, he should go to a fast-food restaurant like the McDonald's down the street, but he shouldn't eat here."

I intuitively knew, but failed to act on, the knowledge that many French chefs and their senior staff view their work as art, not merely food preparation. They take great pride in preparing the fare, ensuring perfect taste and temperature, crafting the presentation, and serving it up with superior service. The diner is expected to savor and enjoy the total experience, not just eat the food. To have it scoffed down would be an insult to their artwork.

I stayed and savored the experience. I could have made that same request at any of the finest restaurants in New York, London, or Tokyo and no one's feelings would have been hurt. But in France, it was simply not done.

It's All Relative

People sometimes categorize New Yorkers as being harsh and abrasive. If you feel the New York style is a little too caustic for you, let me caution you about traveling to Tel Aviv. Israelis have one rule for business etiquette—tell it like it is. Israel is no place to ask, "Do these pants make me look fat?" unless you're ready to hear the harsh truth.

When doing business in Israel, prepare for a mask-free style of play. More important advice: if your native culture avoids confrontation, you may want to leave that approach at home; here you may be perceived as deceptive or pandering. They may allow special dispensation knowing your background, but you certainly won't win any friends or allies in the conference room.

Londoners have a keen ear for accents, which define class and place of birth. And from Cockney to Palace British, the level spoken can define the level of service you receive. All countries have their subcultures or regions that pull rank to be superior. In the United States, there are lessons to learn in order to better communicate across what we might call regional tribes as well as corporate cultures.

We'll talk more about global micromessaging in Chapter 13. In the next chapter we'll examine the tribal differences within the United States that separate East Coast from West Coast, the north from the south, liberals from conservatives, and sales from human resources—even those folks on the fifth floor from those on the ninth.

CHAPTER 8

Speaking the Language

W hen in Rome, do as the Romans do. When in Rome, Georgia,...say, "Y'all." That first segment is an old addage that is well understood. It's the second half that can be the downfall of our more frequent regional encounters. When obvious cultural differences exist, our awareness of them is heightened. When the differences are more subtle and closer to home, they are easily overlooked as is the significance of their impact on relationships.

When preparing for business meetings in Rome, Italy, I give careful thought to the behaviors that increase or minimize being treated as an outsider. Of course, not all Italian business cultures are the same. There are, however, behaviors, styles, and customs common to regions and cultures. Greeting a stranger with a double-cheek kiss and hug in Chicago may not result in the same endearing response as it receives in Latin America.

As odd as it may feel to a Northerner, a couple well-placed "Y'alls" while breaking the ice with folks in the South, may begin to melt away the regional "us/them" barrier. If you're thinking it might seem a little pretentious, don't! At least no more pretentious than abandoning your own language for a well-placed, *merci, gracias*, or *arigato* in worlds where such replacement is ingratiating and appreciated.

Effective fluency isn't *selling out*—it's *fitting in*. It's certainly no revelation that speaking French while conducting a meeting in Paris will likely get you further along than presenting in English. Of course, it isn't just the literal language that fuels comfort and acceptance but also an understanding of and sensitivity to the social mores. The real skill comes in knowing what to look for and what to do with the information. It's just a matter of speaking the language, literally and figuratively. The better we do it, the more we break down barriers of social resistance.

The more we have in common, the more others see us as familiar, and familiarity often gets you invited into that comfortable place where your remarks are respectfully heard, valued, and taken seriously. Demonstrating an understanding of another culture's unique qualities fuels the motivation for acceptance. Speaking the language, in its broadest sense, is far more than the conventional knowledge of word translation. It is a solvent that neutralizes differences allowing even disparate substances to comfortably blend.

Neurolinguistic programming (NLP) for decades has enabled salespeople to win deals that would otherwise have been lost to the competition. The NLP process starts with teaching the skill to analyze the communication styles and behaviors of others. Then the process develops one's skill to effectively replicate selected traits of the other person. If you're imagining some sort of Simon-says skit, don't go there. It's not a mocking or parrot game but simply more like speaking the language of the other person.

> Demonstrating an understanding of another culture's unique qualities fuels the motivation for acceptance.

The NLP analysis looks for key behavioral styles. Does the person you are speaking with use analogies in his or her speech pattern? Is humor often laced into the person's remarks? Does the person ask questions or prefer doing the telling? Is the person's style hard and matter of fact or softer and chatty? Hand gestures, eye contact, or even sentence structure and sequencing of remarks provide information about an individual's neurolinguistic style preferences. It's these preferences that enable NLPers to "speak the language" in a fluent and familiar way. Effective use of NLP sets a stage of comfort and relaxation for the other person. The normal protective barriers get lowered, and you are more likely welcomed in.

Neurolinguistic programming teaches that we must not judge the differences we observe. All too often our analysis of the differences results in a qualitative assessment of other people. After all, if it's not done the way we do things, how good could it possibly be? NLP is a tool to enhance communication and relationship effectiveness.

> *Neurolinguistic programming teaches that we must not judge the differences we observe.*

This became particularly clear some years ago when I was asked to take on a project in addition to my regular workload. The special assignment had me collaborating with a woman named Jane at the company's office in Monroe, Louisiana. I, however, was in New York City, 1,300 miles away geographically and 13 million miles away in operating style.

Over the course of the twelve weeks we worked together on the project, we never met but did have more than thirty lengthy one-on-one phone meetings. After the first few conversations things became quite chatty. We talked about politics, personal interests, current events, and family. We even shared medical advice when one of us was ill. The project ended and each of us went back to our day jobs.

About a month or so passed when, at a large department-wide meeting in New York, I noticed a woman I didn't know staring at my name tag. She had a huge grin and was pointing to her own name tag. She slowly stepped forward and introduced herself. It was my Monroe colleague from the special project, Jane.

Pointing at my name tag, she read it as if to inform me who I was, "You're Steve Young. I'm Jane!" she exclaimed in a bouncy, excited voice.

I smiled, but just as I began to extend my arm to shake, she threw both arms around me. I might add this was not your routine, barely-even-touch-one-another business hug. This was an arms-wrapped-around, pull-tight, damn-it's-good-to-see-you embrace. While she's squeezing me, I was thinking, in my New York head, "What *is* this woman doing?" I was sure my Wall Street buddies observing this passionate display were all wondering the same thing. However, Jane was behaving perfectly appropriately for someone from Monroe, Louisiana. Conversely, had I relocated to Monroe and proceeded to operate in the cool, "urban-professional" manner that passes for normalcy on Wall Street, I would be the one who would be perceived as odd. There I would be seen as the cold, distant, arrogant New Yorker—though it wouldn't at all reflect who I really am.

Each of us carries patterns of behavior and interpretation that takes decades to learn. It is our cultural template. Everyone intellectually knows that behaviors vary across geographic regions. But when we actually find ourselves thrown into a culture vastly different from our own, intellect meets reality and we briefly go into culture shock. What I failed to appreciate from my Monroe colleague was that her hugs sprang from her cultural template. Of course, she was guilty of doing exactly the same thing by not recognizing mine. As in global cross-cultural relations, the takeaway here is that the *sender*, in this case Jane, is the one who defines the accuracy of a message. Your interpretation may be different but the sender defines what is *really* being said.

I wasn't being too cold, and Jane wasn't being too warm. Neither of us had adjusted our cultural filters to best build the business relationship. What a loss!

Of course, we establish ways of interpreting behaviors from a very early age. We watch the way those around us behave, react, and speak and, regardless of their words, figure out the true meaning. We develop an ethnocentric bias we are hardly aware of, driving how we filter the behaviors of everyone we encounter. Simply stated, most of us believe our way is "right," and we tend to judge others by how they measure up to our standards. We often disregard reality and see what we want.

> *Everyone intellectually knows that behaviors vary across geographic regions. But when we actually find ourselves thrown into a culture vastly different from our own, intellect meets reality and we briefly go into culture shock.*

Cultural Interpretations

I learned a few more lessons from Jane. Because she was one of the several people in her group for whom it was a first visit to New York, I thought I'd give them a taste of the quintessential New York experience—a New York deli sandwich. I trotted everyone to one of my favorite midtown delis. After we'd ordered and were waiting for our sandwiches, Jane turned to me and whispered, "Do you believe how obnoxious that guy was behind the counter?" Ready to come to her defense I innocently asked, "What happened?"

"You didn't notice?" Jane asked. "We were hardly through the door when…" She stopped to demonstrate what happened. Jane snapped her fingers a few times; she then wagged her finger at me, in a "come on, let's go, let's go" gesture. Then, in a fairly decent imitation of a Brooklyn accent, she mimicked, "Hey, hey, whaddya want?"

For anyone familiar with lunch hour in midtown Manhattan, you'll understand the only proper response to Jane. "And...?" I asked, perplexed about what had gone wrong.

Jane explained that if a shopkeeper in Monroe behaved that way toward customers, he'd be out of business in a flash. "Anyone behind a counter providing service in my world always connects personally with their customers. The small talk can be anything from the weather to local politics—or just asking how someone's day is going. It is basic civility," Jane said. She made it clear that no store in her neighborhood could survive in business without it—no matter how good or how inexpensive their products. Business people in Monroe know that cordial intimacy with a customer engenders customer loyalty, she finished.

I explained to Jane how the deli counterman had done our region's version of "cordial intimacy" as well. It was exactly what was expected in my world. He knows that I'm in a hurry. I want my sandwich—the quicker the better. It's superficial, pretentious, and really none of *his* business how my day is going so far anyway. The deli guy's actions were the norm for the city. He was operating within the cultural template of Manhattan, where speed is associated with the quality of service.

When I rattled off my request for a "cornedbeefonryetomatoeswithRussian" without taking a breath, and without taking more of his time and mine by adding a "please," I had identified myself as one of his cultural brethren.

The fact that I'd dispensed with any superficial niceties meant we were speaking the same language. He knew that what was most important to me was that I get my sandwich as soon as possible—nothing personal. And, in fact, my order came several minutes ahead of Jane's, who was no doubt labeled as an outsider when she sent the deli guy her own micromessage about his needing a little work on his manners.

Regional culture includes the unwritten rules of the social games we play, and these extend very easily into the business setting. People who travel within the United States quickly pick up on the differences in communication styles from regional

Regional culture includes the unwritten rules of the social games we play, and these extend very easily into the business setting.

to region. Certainly, the more we become aware and respectful of these differences, the easier transactions between regions become.

Left Coast, Right Coast

For example, if you've done business on both U.S. coasts, you are aware of a different communication dynamic and general style. Each coast has its own way of describing how it perceives itself and the other coast's behaviors. A Californian presenting to an audience of native New Yorkers usually stands out like an orange in a bowl of big apples. Though easily noticed, the micromessages that define the differences are predictably tricky to describe. Many New Yorkers returning to the East after working in Los Angeles, where they stood out like apples, find, for reasons they don't quite understand, that they were perceived as difficult to work with. Few can precisely describe what created the tension, but the micromessages revealed all and shaped how the person was viewed.

"We must never assume we are fully aware of what we communicate to someone else," the anthropologist Edward T. Hall wrote in his classic text, *The Silent Language.* "There exist in the world today tremendous distortions in meaning, as people try to communicate with one another. The job of achieving insight and understanding into mental processes of others is much more difficult than most of us care to admit," Dr. Hall wrote this almost a half-century ago.[1]

What is true for understanding and communicating across regional cultural gaps is also true for communicating within a single corporate culture. When you step into a new job, you need to learn how the regional and corporate cultures manifest themselves in that environment. Businesses spawn jargon, style, behavior, and other cultural norms, which individuals joining the organization need to learn and decide whether to conform to. A new hire's compliance to the cultural norms signals to others that he or she is a member of the "tribe," someone "in the know," and connected.

Conformance should never violate your personal values. If the conformity is within the range of acceptability, it can be leveraged to enhance the business experience. Operating in an overly friendly fashion in a conservative business environment, where a reserved manner is prevalent, can be as ineffective as the stuffed shirt working in the more relaxed, highly interactive, looser atmosphere that came of age in the dot-com era.

Conformance should never violate your personal values. If the conformity is within the range of acceptability, it can be leveraged to enhance the business experience.

Does this mean that we have to be disingenuous to be effective? Absolutely not. To be a more authentic business leader in the context of your own business culture does not require putting on a mask. No one likes a phony. The goal is to operate within your own range of flexibility without compromising personal values. We learn to become aware of the cultural language and system of symbols and manners, and we use them as best we can to communicate well and to get the job done.

---

[1] Edward T. Hall, *The Silent Language.* New York: Anchor Books/Random House, 1959, 1990.

Verbalize and Validate

Many leaders are too narrow about their flex range, even when minor adjustments could have a major impact on the performance of their teams and the business. When they sense a particular employee doesn't conform to their own style, that employee gets sent microinequities that can make the staffer feel alienated and probably less willing to perform up to his or her potential. For example, if a conservative manager feels uncomfortable with the clothing style of a staffer, that manager might send micromessages of disapproval.

When we perceive an action that is interpreted as offensive, we have a responsibility to verbalize and validate.

If a visiting manager from a region with a more relaxed style greets the more conservative senior executive with slap on the shoulder as he would in his home office, the superior may interpret the action as insubordinate and inadvertently send subtle messages making his feelings known.

The mistake in both instances is that the receiver has not learned to read the message through the eyes of the sender. Everyone carries within themselves cultural patterns which they've acquired over a lifetime. The true leader takes the time to observe, ask questions, learn, and operate through the filter of "where the other guy is coming from." When we perceive an action that is interpreted as offensive, we have a responsibility to verbalize and validate.

The sender of the message becomes responsible for confirming or modifying the message to make clear what was intended.

The receiver has the primary responsibility for resolving a potential misinterpretation. The receiver must take the initiative and *verbalize* how a particular message was interpreted, facilitating a process that will *validate* the accuracy of the message. The receiver of the message passes the baton. The sender of the message becomes responsible for confirming or modifying the message to make clear what was intended.

It is a process that gets to the core meaning of a message and allows us all to speak the same workplace and social language.

What's in It for Me?

"**Y**ou're the microinequities guy, right?" asked one of three men who approached me in the cafeteria of their office building. (I have accepted my name is far less memorable to people than the experience.) I nod yes. "You know what? You might be responsible for turning our entire office around," he tells me.

Their parent company, a national bank, was about a year into a merger with another major regional bank. The merger had gotten off to a rocky start in their department. Anyone who has gone through the emotional, social, and personal stress of a merger will strongly identify with their perspective. "We were on the wrong side of the merger," his friend chimed in. "The person appointed to head our team came from the *other* side," he snickered. "We got constant microinequities from our new boss that said, 'You're not from my original team, I'll put up with you, but you're not part of my original family. And don't screw up!'"

It was clear to all three of the men that the negative vibe they felt was being directed solely at them, the ones from the other heritage company. In contrast, the guys who had migrated with the manager were golden—they could do no wrong. "It was all as subtle as those examples you showed us, so there was nothing we could say," one of them recalled. They explained how the subtlety was so camouflaged that the three of them never spoke to each other about what they were feeling. Yet they each, independently, had similar reactions to the situation, causing them to shut down on the job. In team meetings they always played the safe role. They never challenged, nor did anything that would deviate from the "group think." But none of them were able to point to anything in particular the new manager was doing to cause their shift in attitude.

Unfortunately, the micromessages they had been receiving were not limited to their manager. Several other team members had picked up on the manager's style and jumped on the bandwagon. Although it presumably had nothing to do with the three men, the increased number of team members echoing the boss's behavior made a bad situation worse. But who could blame the others for following in his footsteps? It's human nature to gravitate to places of comfort and safety. To be securely tucked under the manager's wing is a safe and comfortable place to be. No one gets to the next level within an organization, skill aside, unless your immediate boss respects and likes you. By emulating his behavior, the other team members were getting in his good graces.

While the principal prerequisite for assuming a new assignment is skill of execution (although history has proven that even skill may not be necessary for success), *respect* and *like* are two other critical components in the equation. Respect involves general admiration on the part of those around you. Being *liked*, however, is even more important, believe it or not. No matter what else you've got, if your manager doesn't like you, you can pretty much hang it up. Speaking up and voicing occasional disagreement, is a good thing—it shows your strength and independent thought—but constant opposition with the boss can be a risky proposition that can lead to animosity and dislike. However, be careful not to be a panderer.

Based on their boss's treatment of them, all three of these men figured they were simply being overly sensitive. Since none of them could articulate exactly what they were feeling, maybe it just wasn't there, they each thought. So they left it alone, because they each felt incapable of convincing others of what they were sensing. They thought they would look awfully foolish trying to convince someone else to see and understand something even they couldn't fully describe.

Those three male banking executives explained how everything changed once they learned the process of identifying, articulating, and confronting micromessages. "Our manager sat through your seminar with us," one of them said. And they detected an early wind of change even before leaving that session. As scenarios were discussed that just happened to illustrate many of his own behaviors, the manager would occasionally glance over at them, revealing embarrassment and defensiveness.

Once back on the job, the men weren't surprised that the manager's original team members continued to receive preferential treatment, but something was different. His face told them that the message about micromessages and its impact on performance was hitting home. They finally decided to pull the trigger and take action.

The next time the manager became impatient with their input at a meeting, while he tolerated the long-winded solutions from the members of his original team, the three guys asked the question, very comfortably, without missing a beat, "Was that a microinequity?"

One of the important strategies they learned from the session was to phrase the concern in the form of a question—not an accusation. The manager, no dummy, connected their observations with the epiphany they had experienced in the classroom where he'd recognized the damages inflicted by microinequities. Originally, the manager had been resistant to attending yet another group training experience, but it was evident, particularly to our trio, that he vividly remembered how the microinequities thrown at him during the class caused his own performance to wither. He saw the real damage micromessages could do. On the surface, he had always wanted to bring the two legacy groups together, but something was operating below the ground level causing an *us* versus *them* territorial battle. The microinequities workshop was the beginning of the end of that war.

"It's never been the same for the three of us since," the third man offered, who until that point had been silent, letting his colleagues tell the story. "It only took a couple of days, and everything started to feel different. I've even started reaching out to the people on the other side and stopped treating them like adversaries. Even though we come from different sides, for the first time, the entire group is thriving as a team!" He was on a roll, "What has fundamentally changed is that now we can call it when we see it. We always felt it, but couldn't comfortably articulate it. Now we have a lexicon to describe it. The term *microinequities* gave us a legitimate platform for shining a bright light on the things that were shrouded in ambiguity. Now, in virtually every meeting, we strip away the outer shells and get to the essence of what is really going on. Believe me, work is getting done very differently now."

Those who have historically been the perpetrators of microinequities (microperps) or who, at the very least, have rarely been on the receiving end of microinequities, are more prone to dismiss them. Traditional diversity schemes tell managers what to do and how to behave. In turn, managers follow those directives, but rarely see value for their efforts. Instead, they see what amounts to a new form of affirmative action, disguised under the banner of yet another euphemism: "diversity." This sort of struc-

> *The term* microinequities *gave us a legitimate platform for shining a bright light on the things that were shrouded in ambiguity.*

ture is the single most important reason that so many corporate diversity efforts flounder or fail.

Diversity Misperceptions

A diversity *malaise* has seeped into the landscape of corporate culture. In many organizations, diversity functions as a necessary "must have," but is often perceived as a sort of philanthropic or legal function striving to make things pleasant and comfortable for the underrepresented, while protecting the company's legal liabilities. Unfortunately, those who see the function through that lens have not only missed the boat, but will likely be stuck on the island indefinitely.

How can you truly be an effective leader, if you can't *effectively* manage everyone on your team? The real power of diversity is the skill of identifying what is unique about each member of the team, and applying specific developmental and motivational strategies that amplify each individual's performance. Until you are able to identify the unique characteristics that motivate people differently, and apply that awareness as a catalyst to generate maximum commitment, support, collaboration, loyalty, and performance from the entire team, you cannot be a truly great leader.

Diversity may have its origins in the desire to fix a social problem, but its real power is its ability to *ignite stars*. It takes considerable effort to identify the unique profiles of your staff, but do you really believe there's any chance of getting different people to their peak levels using one single management style? Not likely.

The many successful leaders who used a singular style, regardless of their ultimate success, were performing at a level of oblivious mediocrity. Their success would no doubt have soared to greater heights if they had applied their ample leadership skills to the unique needs of the individual. But there is no incentive to adopt

> *The real power of diversity is the skill of identifying what is unique about each member of the team, and applying specific developmental and motivational strategies that amplify each individual's performance.*

a different style if you don't see a need or reason to change.

Diversity initiatives will only become successful when the people who dominate the positions of power and influence see and feel how the process has a long-term personal benefit for them. Not much in the world of business ever reaches levels of success until those holding the reins clearly see: *What's in it for me?*

What's in it for you is mastering the link between leadership and performance. When this is achieved, even staunch disbelievers switch from being "pulled" to "pushing" hard in favor of the effort.

This expanded definition of diversity includes factors like the way you talk, how long you've been with the company, how you dress, wear your hair, and even whether you have a tattoo, none of which help define the quality of what you bring to the organization. However, they do, in many cases, alter how well you are accepted and treated at work. These judgments, which we all make at one time or another, serve to divide us into ready-made camps of "Them" and "Us." Which, scientists say, is actually quite natural.

In his classic text *The Nature of Prejudice*, psychologist Gordon W. Allport explained that each of us has to find a way to order the world around us and our needs.[1] Dividing things—including people—into categories is one of the things we do to feel we have control of our lives.

To say that prejudice has its roots in human nature is not to excuse it. But it helps to know that everyone harbors bias; and more often than not, bias is applied to things rather than people. Our prejudice, "prejudging," is making assumptions without having

---

[1] Gordon W. Allport, *The Nature of Prejudice*. Addison-Wesley, 1954, 1979.

adequate information. Making assumptions based on past experience can actually hamper our growth and success.

For instance, you stop buying takeout at a place because it once sold you spoiled food. But the establishment may have changed hands and the cuisine there may be excellent now, but you'll never know. You assume it's the same. What you do know is you don't want to get sick again. Or you may use a mechanic who has done a good job in the past on your car even if a new garage opens up closer to where you live. You assume yours is still the better choice, without even exploring your other options.

> *Making assumptions based on past experience can actually hamper our growth and success.*

But more serious prejudices, unfortunately, are also universal. We rely heavily on the assumptions we've been culturally conditioned to accept, says Harvard psychologist Mahzarin R. Banaji. Professor Banjo has developed a system to measure implicit prejudices—the ones that come with being born into a particular culture. And the news is not good.

Professor Banaji asked subjects to use a computer keypad to quickly tap their response to photos of a variety of people—black, white, old, fat, gay, attractive, male, and female. She found that when forced to quickly make a judgment on appearance, most people—including those with liberal politics—associate black, gay, fat, and old with "bad," and attractive, white men with "good."[2]

These are the sorts of judgments that come into play in the workplace, and while they may not inspire macroinequities, they are the birthing place for the many micromessages we send routinely without knowing it.

In the case of the bank merger team members, the difference in the way they were treated had nothing to do with any of what I like

---

[2] M. R. Banaji and R. Bhaskar. "Implicit Stereotypes and Memory: The Bounded Rationality of Social Beliefs." In D. L. Schachter and E. Scarry (Eds.). *Memory, Brain, and Belief.* Cambridge, MA: Harvard University Press, 2000, pp. 139–175.

to call the "elephant-sized" factors we have been trained to watch for—issues like race, gender, or sexual orientation. Rather, the disparity stemmed from the subtle, "ant-sized" distinctions of which side of the merger the men had been on.

In this case, the recipients of microinequities were three white men working in corporate America, demonstrating quite clearly that anyone can be on the receiving end of a microinequity. Under the terms of traditional diversity, these white men should have been immune from suffering. However, that was not the case. The microinequity messages they received from their boss deeply impaired their performance, directly influencing productivity and the success of the new team.

> Whether the problem is elephant-sized or ant-sized, the first step in addressing the micromessages we send and receive is to become aware of them.

Whether the problem is elephant-sized or ant-sized, the first step in addressing the micromessages we send and receive is to become aware of them. All of us send and receive micromessages. Our mission is to identify when we send, receive, or observe these messages, and how best to adjust the elements we control in order to alter the outcomes.

CHAPTER 10

Retrain Your Brain

A lthough everyone has his or her performance affected by micromessages, some are affected disproportionately. Women, people of color, and those with disabilities seem to get more than average microinequities. As Maureen Walker, Ph.D., Associate Director, the Harvard Business School, once said to me, "When we show up, we arrive in a body." People see us and promptly put us through a series of mental filters or checklists. The body we arrive in is what people most readily see: our race, gender, age, attractiveness, and other items that define our visible profile.

The first thing mammals identify is gender. Dogs aren't exactly discreet in the way they determine this, but it is their first order of business. People often become frozen when they can't identify a person's gender. They attempt to reconcile the seemingly conflicting signals of body shape, voice frequency, hair length, facial hair, and other distinguishing factors, to the detriment of any conversation they might have been having.

The second step on our mental checklist is to assess whether the person is generally like us in structure. Here, we identify whether someone uses a wheelchair, is extraordinarily tall or exceptionally small, is missing a limb, or has some other significantly different physical characteristic. Next is race. And it's not just Black noticing White, or vice versa, it's also noticed intraracially. Skin tone and color tell us about how much we are alike or different, even within the same race.

Culture or nationality likely place fourth in sequence on the checklist. If the average acculturated American were to sit down for an intimate chat with a Korean, an Aboriginal Australian, an Egyptian, a Hawaiian, or a Nigerian, even if they were of similar skin colors, the American may suffer a debilitating brain freeze.

When groups come together, the checklist process is highly active, as members compare and contrast those around them. It is the central theme of all first dates. How that checklist gets tallied by the end of the evening determines whether there will be a second date.

> *The micromessages we choose to send others are influenced by the elements on our individual checklists.*

The micromessages we choose to send others are influenced by the elements on our individual checklists. Some of the items come with a person at birth and are beyond our control, while others represent our life choices. We are born with race and gender, but we choose style and behavior, for example. How we assess each item on the checklist influences the micromessages we send and receive.

A Microinequities Primer: Ms. Davis's Story

Ms. Andrea Davis, a middle-aged, African-American woman, is a very successful investment banker with a husband who owns a local business. They do very well financially. They live in a very impressive, affluent home—I'm not talking about your nice four-bedroom, two-car garage home—this is what most would call an estate. The Davis estate includes acres of land, a guest house, swimming pool, tennis courts. You get the picture.

Ms. Davis told me that it is quite common for her to arrange for a worker or company to come to her home to take care of repairs or home improvements. But she is usually never there to receive them. There are people who handle these matters in her absence, since she is always at the office Monday through Friday. But occasionally, the contractors, designers, or caterers arrive on a Saturday, when she is there to personally speak with them. She described what that experience has been like.

She opens the door, the contractor looks at her briefly, then looks past her while asking, "Is Ms. Davis home?" Often they are already scanning the hallway behind her for the person they perceive to be their client.

"Of course, as soon as I tell them *I* am Ms. Davis, everything changes," she says. "I get all the respect I deserve. Even all the respect I could imagine. And I tell myself that I was just being oversensitive again."

But two days after attending the MicroInequities program, the very next Saturday, she opened the door to one more nongreeting: "Is Ms. Davis home?" There was no "Hi," "Hello," or "Good morning," not even a wave. There was also no eye contact with her because the man at the door was searching for the person who really owns this place.

She said, at first, she did what she always did—that is, "smile on the outside while cringing inside." But the discussion from the program was still resonating in her head and she found herself thinking, "Listen to all those microinequities." She described his tone of voice as flat, even a bit condescending. His facial expression was cold and for a brief moment he looked at her as if he were actually looking *through* her instead.

There was no introduction, no mention of his company, or why he was there. Obviously, his checklist had concluded that she couldn't possibly be Ms. Davis.

"So I did what you said to do," she told me. "No berating or bludgeoning the guy with the facts about his racial predisposition. Instead, I simply sat him down and asked him questions and gave him a brief primer on microinequities. Well, let's just say, he'll never do it again."

The reason why might surprise you. She did her best to keep both anger and guilt-tripping out of their interaction. Instead, she very calmly ran through the microinequities and micromessages he had unwittingly conveyed. Because she'd learned how accusations put someone on the defensive, she chose instead to itemize the tiny signals of disrespect in his behavior. Approaching him as one human being to another, she felt that he did not feel threatened, and she sensed that all this would have a positive impact on him with future clients.

This may be a chance for you to test yourself. What were the microinequities that Andrea observed in that brief exchange and what exactly did each mean? In those four brief words (Is Ms. Davis home?), there were about a dozen microinequities. Are you able to identify them?

No doubt you'll find this a struggle. Although we might now be better prepared to begin pointing them out, people still find it difficult to put their finger on the details of what effect this terse exchange likely had on Ms. Davis.

Microinequities comprise two components: the message itself and what the message means. In her case, the eye movement revealed several messages. First, that he had no interest in dealing with her. Second, she was not worthy of his time, and, third, and most obviously, that she was not Ms. Davis. It was a conclusion reached by the subtleties in his facial expression, tone of voice, choice of words, eye movement, lack of greeting, and no mention of who he was and why he was there. All things he would have done differently if he knew he was speaking to his client.

Thanks to his vapid facial expression, she felt exactly zero social connection. For many of us, there are lots of people with whom we must routinely interact, though we have no desire to connect with them on a personal level. An almost universal example is the taxi driver with whom we share a ride but find little reason to engage in conversation. Do not fool yourself into believing this has anything to do with the driver being a stranger you will never see again. Replace the driver and test that theory.

Microinequities comprise two components: the message itself and what the message means.

How would you behave during a shared ride with a commuter you didn't know? Riding into the city for twenty or thirty minutes with another complete stranger who, just like the driver, you will likely never see again. It is unlikely you would sit there and not engage in some respectful, albeit forced and usually dull, conversation. The underlying reason for the disconnection with the driver is entirely influenced by the driver's subservient role.

The same is true of the waitstaff in restaurants. People don't generally respond to the waitress in the same way they respond to the restaurant owner who stops by the table to ask how things are. The owner is an equal, the waitress is subservient.

My friend, Ms Davis, was immediately put in the lesser ranks of those providing service. After all, in the contractor's mind, this lady in the doorway was nothing more than another obstacle in his path to Ms. Davis. So he thought he would cut out a step and try to find the real Ms Davis himself by looking past her.

Even the sentence structure itself was revealing, "Is Ms. Davis home?" Think about it. Is that how you would greet the person you knew was Ms. Davis? Go ahead: conjure up a stereotype. Maybe a middle-aged white woman wearing a St. John's outfit, hair fixed to be impervious to hurricane, impressive jewelry, holding a little Maltese dog. *This* is Ms. Davis. There she is.

Pretend that you are the contractor. The bell rings, the door opens, and there she stands. The hair, outfit, jewelry, and the little dog: check, check, check, and check. You know you are looking at Ms. Davis, so you extend your hand, make eye contact, smile, and say, "Good morning, Ms. Davis. I am Bob the Builder. I'm here about the deck." The facial expression, tone of voice, gestures, choice of words, all instantly fall into line when you know you are dealing with the "right" person.

This story is all too common in the workplace. When we make assumptions in the workplace, we impair performance. Imagine someone approaching your desk and giving you the first version of this Davis experience. The microinequities are endless. Now compare that to the microadvantage of saying, "Hi," extending a hand, and saying, "Good morning. I'm Bob. Are you the person I will be working with on this project?"

When we make assumptions in the workplace, we impair performance.

This case simply underscores the fact that, although everyone knows subtle messages exist, we need to go a level deeper to understand what they are, how often we send them, and what their effect is on the recipient. Most importantly, we need to know that by making slight adjustments to the messages we send, we are able to have a profound effect on the reaction, response, and performance of our receivers. In the workplace, people send messages that let you know where they think you belong in the hierarchy. The messages confirm that you are beneath or at my level and determine you deserve my respect.

As natural as it may be to use the checklist to assess the people we interact with, it no longer serves its mammalian purposes in a high-technology, global, twenty-first century. We don't need to fear that the people we interact with may be members of a neighboring and dangerous tribe. Today our tribe could include twenty people on a conference call from multiple countries, stretching several time zones, looking dramatically different, yet with the same family (company) name.

Let the checklist operate as information only. Remove it from your filters and use the precision of micromessages for your lens instead.

Assess tone of voice, facial expression, gestures, proximity, and eye contact, a person's choice of words, syntax, and nuance, along with all indicators of what the message is conveying beneath the words themselves. This practice will identify the true messages being sent and how best to respond. Since it's always the cultural template of the sender that defines the accuracy of the message, using this process still requires constant validation of your assumptions.

Mastery of this skill minimizes the gap of actions based on miscommunication and strengthens relationships to support productivity.

Those who have habitually received a disproportionate share of microinequities are often more aware of their existence and eager to respond when they occur. But as radar becomes more finely tuned to the stealth delivery of microinequities you will begin to see how no one is immune.

CHAPTER 11

Is This About Faking It?

I was waiting in the wings while the head of U.S. operations for a major multinational company introduced me as the featured speaker for the day's meeting. Bill had attended one of my sessions and then called me in to speak to his executive team several months later. This was the company's annual senior leadership meeting: the top 1 percent, the crème de la crème of the corporate hierarchy. The audience included some 500 corporate leaders from around the globe.

Bill's introduction was a warm story of his personal epiphany about micromessaging, brought on by his participation in a previous session with me. He told the audience how the work we did helped him revise his way of interacting with clients and colleagues—and even his family. My face was beaming, my chest puffed out, as I waited for the flattering introduction to end, so I could go on stage. But I was awakened from my dreamlike state by what Bill said next. "Yes, listening to Steve really did change my life. But for the first few weeks after we met, I really hated Steve's guts." The smile on my face fell and my heart dropped.

Bill went on to explain, in great detail, exactly why he hated my guts. For the first month after he'd been in my seminar, he had become obsessed with micromessages. Here was the head of U.S. operations confessing to what was, essentially, his corporate royal court that our work together had made him self-conscious, not only about what he was saying, but how he said it. And the more he talked about it, the angrier at me he seemed.

"I'm sitting through meetings," he told the audience, "trying to figure out if I've smiled as much at one employee as I have to another one. I'd ask myself if I committed a microinequity when I said, 'great idea,' to one person, but only, 'thank you' to someone else. When I jotted down notes while one person spoke, but listened attentively to another team member's idea, had I sent one a microadvantage? Focusing on these micromessages was driving me nuts. I was the boss! But I was walking on eggshells, focusing more on process than content."

> *Managing micromessages well is about being equitable—fair—not identical.*

Mercifully, his remarks finally turned a corner. "Well, it took me that month to begin to understand that becoming aware of the micromessages we send—which Steve is going to tell you all about—is not about sending false messages. It's not about doing it the same way for everyone."

In those two sentences he captured the practice that had him walking on eggshells during the month after our training. He figured out the process: Managing micromessages well is about being equitable—fair—not identical. It is also about being genuine—saying what is true—without inhibiting performance. "It took me about that first month for micromessaging to become second nature to me. Now I apply it to every meeting, whether with colleagues, friends, or family, and it has made me a far better leader."

> *To maximize your leadership effectives you do not need to focus on being nice or sending microadvantages; you just need to avoid microinequities.*

Applying the micromessaging concepts in no way compromises one's integrity or personal values. To maximize your leadership effectives you do not need to focus on being nice or sending microadvantages; you just need to avoid microinequities. The goal is to maximize leadership effectiveness while remaining true to your personal, authentic self.

Authentic and Honest

The following is an example of how, as a manager, you can deliver a message that is in no way kind or nice but that completely avoids microinequities.

Assume someone on a manager's team delivered a truly awful presentation. The manager might approach that person and say, with a neutral facial expression and a firm but nonsuggestive tone of voice, "George, your presentation was extremely poor. You were expected to present topics A, B, and C and instead, you covered D, E, and F. Several people came in from a number of sites for this presentation, all with a specific set of expectations. I think they all felt that it was a waste of their time, and I agree. And frankly, it was a waste of my time as well. This cannot happen again. The next time you do a presentation, I want to see an outline in advance. I would like to review the content of what you are going to present, and I want to see you deliver a sample portion of the presentation as well. This was clearly substandard, and we cannot have anything like this happen again."

Obviously, the manager's remarks were nothing that anyone would want to hear from his or her manager. But, as unpleasant as it was, there were no microinequities in the delivery—nothing to suggest the comments were anything more than professionally driven. Contrast this with an alternative approach laden with microinequities.

The manager sees George in the hallway after the presentation and begins to walk toward him with a dismayed look on his face. Hands on hips, he stops suddenly and stares at him. Then, rather than say anything constructive, he emits a deep "hrrumph," throws his arms down so his hands slap his thighs. He shakes his head from side to side, like he's saying no, as though there is nothing that can be done, and then he turns and walks the other way.

Although the first message was harsh, it was something George can recover from because it offers specific directives for improving his performance. No personal assaults occur; the feedback is completely about his performance, not him as a person. The second message, however, though wordless, conveyed emotional baggage that George will be carrying around for some time. With no constructive content, the message delivered said, "You're an embarrassment. I don't want you around. You're hopeless. I've given up on you and you're not worth my time."

The lack of concrete criticism lets George's imagination run wild. He knows his manager is disappointed, but he has been given no specific direction. George knows everything about the manager's feelings toward him, but nothing about what he can do to correct it. There's just no way to recover. So George worries and wonder about it, rather than knowing how to perform differently in the future.

To be helpful and constructive, every negative message must be accompanied by the alternative of what was expected and how far the employee fell from the mark. Even when someone is being terminated for substandard performance, there should be no misunderstanding of why the individual's performance didn't meet your expectations.

A senior-level executive goaded me on this issue by complaining: "There are things I really don't like about a certain person on my team. She doesn't know enough. She talks more than she works. Am I supposed to do 'day care' with her? Tell her 'good job,' even when she, in fact, isn't doing a good job at all? Am I supposed to mask my real feelings, pretend I like the woman when I really can't stand her?"

Let's hit that one head on. No, we don't expect people to violate their values and do things that send inappropriate or wrong messages. We all live with some level of pretense. It comes with being a part of civilization.

Let me use myself as an example. I am personally opposed to the concept of wearing a necktie. It is a superfluous piece of material that neither holds my shirt up nor keeps my neck warm. Occasionally, it acts as an expensive napkin. But it is within the range of what I am willing to do to earn respect and acceptance in certain environments.

As with all business processes, we sometimes must comply with things we may not personally subscribe to or endorse. Of course, my flexibility has its limits. I wouldn't wear lederhosen or a kilt because it falls outside of my range of what I'm comfortable doing, but others might. Managing this process well is about being equitable, not identical. It is also about being genuine—saying what is true—without inhibiting performance.

In another example of being flexible, I came home very late one evening, having traveled all week and then taken the red-eye home from the West Coast. I was exhausted. What I really wanted to do was just unwind by myself and watch some mindless TV. It was in the wee hours of the morning when I put my key in the door and, of course, both of my children were still up waiting for me. Did I say, "Please just leave me alone. I'm exhausted"? Of course not, I smiled and hugged them. I did what every responsible parent would do. I sat down for a visit and listened avidly to the stories of their week. Am I being disingenuous? Faking it? To some degree, yes. But it is a "faking it" that is appropriate and still supports my values.

In the workplace, we have a responsibility to ensure that all employees are given the messages, conditions, and environment to perform to the fullest of their potential—and to unlock talent that runs the risk of being underutilized.

The practical application of the power of micromessages is not about being nice. It is about sending messages that are clear, direct, and fair. We need to understand how even the most subtle nuances of our delivery influences each person getting the messages. Every micromessage a manager sends affects an employee's perceptions of the company. And these perceptions, of course, greatly influence how effective that employee will be while working for the company.

In the workplace, we have a responsibility to ensure that all employees are given the messages, conditions, and environment to perform to the fullest of their potential—and to unlock talent that runs the risk of being underutilized.

This is not just about the chemistry and ambience in our work environment. It's about making sure that each employee is managed in a way that brings out his or her full potential in support of the company. Ultimately, it's about making everyone as productive as possible.

So wear the tie, hug the kids, and if you don't like someone, don't lie. But don't send them micromessages that undermine their performance for your company.

CHAPTER 12

That's One Dumb Rat!

Whenever we interact with a group in a meeting, or with an individual, we walk in carrying our own fixed ideas and filters. It's our baggage, and on these trips you can't go empty-handed. You might be carrying a small under-the-seat tote, or, when you encounter a different group, you may drag along a steamer trunk. Pick your metaphor. Call it baggage, rose-colored versus dark-gray glasses, or some other visualization. All of us have a tendency to reach conclusions based more on our preconceptions than the facts of the encounter itself.

Seeing Is Believing

Expectations quickly become reality, especially when someone we trust shares her perspective or opinion. For instance, you arrive at a hotel that was recommended by a friend who has extraordinarily high standards. You walk in the lobby and immediately notice the impressive wall hangings. On the way to your room, you glance into the hotel restaurant and notice the flowers on

> *Expectations quickly become reality, especially when someone we trust shares her perspective or opinion.*

tables and broad buffet selection. The waiter walking by is smiling and appears to be carrying an impressive bottle of champagne. You conclude you have chosen well.

You continue searching for other indicators that this is the chic place your friend said it would be and that you now believe it is. It might be as insignificant as the shape of the ashtrays in the lobby or how neatly the linens have been folded in your room. Everywhere you look, you find reinforcements of your preconceptions. Even when you find something that seems a bit odd or out of place, you chalk it up to being intentionally unique, rather than substandard.

You might draw open the curtains to discover your view is a brick wall. You smile and chalk it up to the limitations of a big city; in some ways it becomes almost cool. At this point, only something extreme and dramatic could turn your feelings around about your wonderful new find.

On the other hand, if your friend had snubbed the hotel, complaining about its substandard ambiance and services, you would never notice the flowers, buffet, champagne, or neatly folded towels. The artistic ashtrays in the lobby would be little more than a reminder of the discomfort you will likely experience from the smokers.

It's obviously no coincidence what we anticipate often seems to come true; and what we are preconditioned to expect seems to happen. There's more to this than what simply meets the eye, or gut.

Harvard psychologist Robert Rosenthal conducted experiments in the 1960s that showed how people tend to see what they believe, versus believing what they see.[1] Dr. Rosenthal told two sets of students that they were to observe the behavior of rats in a maze. He told half the students that they had the "dumb rats," that is, the ones

---

[1] Robert Rosenthal, "Covert Communication in Classrooms." *EyeonPsichi*, Vol. 3, No. 1 (Fall 1998), pp.18–22.

who had been genetically bred to perform poorly when trying to make their way through a maze. He told the other set of students that they had the "smart rats," bred to excel in maze behavior.

Predictably, the students found exactly what Rosenthal had pre-conditioned them to see. Those who studied the "dumb rats" documented instances of their dullness and lethargy. The students watching the smart rats came back with proof of how the rats were bright, alert, and superbly gifted at finding their way through the maze. They saw what they expected to see, what they believed to be true.

Of course, the rats weren't really bred for anything in particular. For all intents and purposes, they were the same rats. The only "leg up" the so-called smart rats had on their fellow rats was that their judges believed they were better at the task. Were the students stretching the truth to support the professor's conclusion? Probably not. The students simply saw what they *expected* to see. They didn't create evidence that was not there, they simply filtered out any information that ran contradictory to the premise they were trying to prove.

One rat labeled as bright might be moving at a certain speed and suddenly stop. The explanation might be that the rat is carefully pondering what action to take next. The same actions exhibited by a dull rat would likely be seen as confirming its confusion. Such filters do a superb job of catching and filtering out, or in, what we subconsciously expect to see; or making us see what we anticipate.

Filters, in general, are designed to catch certain elements and allow others to pass through. When they are set in place for us they do their jobs quite well. They enable us to turn a blind-eye to what may be staring directly at us. Seeing may be believing, but most of us tend to see what we *already* believe. The filters keep out discrepancies that would upset our point of view. We like to be right.

What if, at the start of the experiment, those two sets of students were riding to class in a taxicab and the driver turned around and said,

> *Seeing may be believing, but most of us tend to see what we already believe.*

"Hey, those rats in the red cage look a lot smarter than the rats in the green cage." It is unlikely the students' conclusions would have been influenced. A manager, much like a professor, exerts an aura of power. His or her directives easily lead employees down the paths predetermined to be of value or importance. The ways in which we set up the filter are largely framed by the person providing perspective, as well as our own expectations. One can be greater than the other, depending upon the reputation of the person providing perspective: taxi driver versus professor.

In a later experiment, Professor Rosenthal proved how a higher authority influenced the way in which teachers filtered their students. More powerfully, he discovered that teachers' expectations profoundly affected student achievement.

At the beginning of a term, teachers were told that certain average students were actually very bright and were expected to perform well. By the end of the semester, the average students were excelling, apparently led to do so by their teacher's expectations. In this case, the filter acted in a positive way. One can imagine the teachers filtering out the mistakes made by these average students, focusing on their behavior that linked them to superior achievement. The average students were unconsciously *pulled ahead* in the academic contest.

This expectation applies equally well in the workplace. If you believe a particular employee is slow and dull-witted, you are likely to habitually filter out most of what he says, believing it is without intellectual merit. But if you have a favorite employee whom you've always admired, it's likely that whenever she utters a remark in a staff meeting, you will either see the brilliance of the comment or ask for help in getting you there.

One illustration of how filters work played out at a major financial institution. Our team's manager had resigned a few months earlier, and the firm had finally hired her replacement. A casual get-to-know-you session had been arranged, where the new manager would be introduced to the team by his boss. Each of us took seats around the conference table and, in standard form, began introducing ourselves and giving a brief description of roles and projects. The team member who had taken on a large part of the management responsibilities over the past months, and was the person most of us felt provided the greatest insight,

If you believe a particular employee is slow and dull-witted, you are likely to habitually filter out most of what he says, believing it is without intellectual merit.

started first. He announced his name, lifted his arm to gesture, and tipped over the manager's coffee. It was his bad luck that the coffee made its way straight to the new manager's stack of papers and his PDA. In a panic, the employee grabbed a stack of napkins and, in an attempt to sop up the spill, pushed the pool of black coffee off the edge and onto our new boss's lap.

The manager was very understanding, or at least he seemed to be. He went on and on saying, "It's no problem. Don't worry about it. It's easy to reprint whatever I need." We were all embarrassed for our friend and were impressed at how accommodating the new guy was.

Unfortunately, during the following weeks and months it became clear that perhaps he hadn't been as understanding as we initially thought. We knew whom he liked and didn't like, with our friend falling in the "didn't like" column. The manager rarely gave him plum projects and seemed to carefully scrutinize each and every presentation he made. Even when there was nothing of significance to criticize, he would find the little stuff—minor typos, formatting inconsistencies. The difference between how he read most presentations and our friend's was that he typically read our submissions for content, but seemed to be proofreading or grading his.

In getting to know the new manager, it became clear he was quite meticulous. Pocket change would be stacked in neat piles by denomination. Pencils had their place with pencils and black and blue pens could be found in separate trays, respectively. The team would joke behind his back that his shirts should be mono-grammed "PAR" for Prince Anal Retentive.

Until our friend transferred to a new area, no one in our group made the connection between that first encounter and the man-ager's subsequent negative views. The clarity came through like a beacon when, several weeks after our friend had left, the manager casually described him as clumsy and disorganized. Nearly all of us had a flashback to that fateful meeting. He had been undone before he ever started. He became the dull rat.

Deciding from the moment we meet a coworker that there is something different or odd about him that makes us feel uncomfortable, we likely implant filters that weed out anything that might make him appealing.

When assessing intangible qualities in our colleagues, like character, mood, or emotion, our filters act powerfully. Deciding from the moment we meet a coworker that there is something dif-ferent or odd about him that makes us feel uncomfortable, we likely implant filters that weed out anything that might make him appealing. We continue to "bank" more and more information, unconscious mes-sages, and signals that support our original belief. Conversely, the peo-ple we like, we, quite simply, cut them a lot of slack.

When we focus on the quantifiable, micromessages get less play. To prove just how much we miss when we focus on something quantifiable, Daniel Simons of the University of Illinois, Urbana, and Christopher Chabris from Harvard University, asked subjects in an experiment to count the number times basketballs were passed from player to player in a prepared videotape.[2] In the video,

---

[2] Daniel Simons and Christopher Chabris. "Gorillas in Our Midst: Sustained Inatten-tional Blindness for Dynamic Events," *Perception*, Vol. 28, pp. 1059–1074.

there are two basketballs and two teams, one in white uniforms, the other in black. Amid their fast air and bounce passes, a person in a gorilla costume walks onto the basketball court, stands among the teams, beats his chest, then walks off.

Following the tape, the subjects were asked for their count of the number of passes; and then asked if they saw anything unusual. Forty-seven percent of the viewers did not see the gorilla and were guilty of what is termed "inattentive blindness." When your visual focus is geared toward one thing, you often miss what is going on around you. It is why you don't see a friend in a movie theater when you are on the hunt for an empty seat, say the researchers. Some of the subjects who had not noticed the gorilla, and who were shown the tape again, believed they were being tricked: that they had been shown two different tapes. This shows how strong these filters can be.

In the same way that filters can interfere with what's really happening, they can control what we think and feel about a particular person. When we meet someone for the first time we can't always quickly decide, based on our traditional elephant-sized criteria of age, race, and gender filters, whether we are dealing with the bright rat or a dull one. However, once we've reached our snap judgment, our filters settle into place, and we look for, and usually find, evidence to back up our assumptions.

I remember screwing up the filters and making a total jerk of myself several years ago when I was working in sales. I had been in the job about five years and was flying high, up there in the top 3 percent of performers. I thought I knew everything. But then the new sales manager showed up. The new sales manager looked twelve years old. What on earth could this *child* teach me? I thought skeptically.

We spent our first day together visiting clients. We returned, I went to my desk, and felt relieved I didn't have to deal with him any longer that day. My phone rang. It was the sales manager. He wanted me to come to his office so he could give me some feedback. Sitting in his office, I only heard Charlie Brown's teacher, "blah, blah, blah...." Though on another level, I was looking and listening carefully for him to say something wrong or make a fool of himself. I was expecting and hoping he would say something stupid. I searched for anything that would validate my preconception.

> *Without distorting the facts, we can distort the vision of what we see to conform to what we believe.*

Was I able to find it? You're damn right I was. Over and over again. After all, he was one of the "dull" rats, so how could I not? My filters were doing their job. If he thought something was half full, I would have seen it as what? Half empty? Wrong. I would have seen it as "almost gone." Without distorting the facts, we can distort the vision of what we see to conform to what we believe.

Each of us goes through his or her version of my encounter with that sales manager in personal and professional relationships every day.

In my case, those filters did get changed. A colleague I greatly admired and respected approached me. My colleague told me, "You're all wrong about this guy. I know him. He's brilliant and deserves all the accolades he's received. This guy's really terrific. You need to give him a fair shot and he's *not* twelve years old." I listened to my colleque, and it didn't take long for me to adjust my filters, and see what I would never have seen otherwise.

Clean Your Filters

You can't deny your innate human filters, but you should override them in the workplace. Unlike the checklist, your filters are often influenced by others.

Robert Rosenthal shaped the perception the students had of their rats and my colleague helped me see what would otherwise have remained invisible.

Our checklists and filters work in concert with one another, although checklists have more to do with compatibility, while filters tell us more about assessment and capability. Performance and compatibility should not be linked. Whether you like, dislike, or are comfortable with someone should not play a role in determining potential, assigning a project, or measuring performance.

Filters are more closely linked to our experiences and the information we receive from others. We should not totally disregard this information, but we do need to clean our filters regularly to make sure we are getting the best possible result.

In some cases, the filters reveal more than the sender may intend. I was conducting the first session of a corporate rollout for a firm of 30,000 employees worldwide. A woman approached me on our first break. Before she spoke, she looked around to make sure no one was listening.

Performance and compatibility should not be linked. Whether you like, dislike, or are comfortable with someone should not play a role in determining potential, assigning a project, or measuring performance.

"So Steve, how did they pick us for this very first session?" she asked. "Does management feel we need it the most? Are we the company's problem children?"

I wondered if she might be a fraction paranoid, but I said, "No. I'm sure it was a random selection process. They wanted people from all departments to sample the seminar."

Then she laughed. "You know, I have learned a lot from you about micromessages today. Whenever you talk to someone, you always maintain deliberate eye contact. And you *were* looking directly at me until you said the word, 'no.' Was there a micromessage there?" She was right. Because when I said, "no," I had begun to wonder if maybe the powers that be had indeed selected the "bad kids." And if they had, I wish they'd told me. I do like to know whom I'm dealing with.

I laughed, caught in my own system. She had read the micromessages perfectly. She had reshaped my filters so that I began to wonder about the connection between the delivery of a first session and any problem or pressing need. I had actually begun to see the group in a different light based on her question. Fortunately, stopping to clean the filters drove us to a discussion with a constructive and clarifying outcome.

CHAPTER 13

Shrink Group Think

If you really want to see microinequities in action, you need go no further than everyday business meetings. As part of my presentations to large groups, I show a video simulation of a team meeting where people send and receive a wide range of micromessages. To an audience that hasn't yet been schooled in the microinequities process, the meeting in the video seems quite typical. Nothing in the video of the meeting seems special. Some things that occur on the tape may stand out as being a bit unusual, but the micromessages that are exchanged represent the sorts of things that we all routinely see in business meetings.

Six of One, Half a Dozen of Another

The scene begins with six people seated around a conference table, waiting for their manager to arrive. As the manager walks into the conference room, he casually, but insincerely, offers apologies for coming late. While walking toward his seat, he stops and whispers a few words to one of the attendees. The manager places his hand on the man's shoulder, and after a few seconds of intimate chat, they both have a friendly laugh.

The manager begins the meeting by getting right to the point. He explains that his mission is to come up with some new suggestions for ways to engage employees. He needs information about the critical issues that concern people, so that the recommended solutions can be brought to senior management. One of the women at the table begins by stating that it is important that whatever strategy comes out of the meeting should include all levels of the organization, and all of the international sites as well.

The manager makes no eye contact while the woman is speaking, offers a very obligatory acknowledgment, and says, "Yes, terrific, thank you."

One of the men then suggests that the strategy needs to be sensitive to vacation schedules. He reminds the team that ensuring the largest volume of participation is critical. The manager's response is to nod affirmatively throughout. At its conclusion, the manager says, "Suneil, actually that's a very good idea. Thank you."

But then he says, "Okay, who wants to get the ball rolling?" The group shows no immediate reaction to the fact that two people have already done just that. Apparently, what they have offered is not what the manager is looking for.

René, seated in the middle of the table, offers her suggestion. She begins by mentioning that she has done quite a bit of research. She goes off on a bit of a preamble about why the idea she will offer is really an effective solution then suggests a series of town hall meetings as a way to get input and perspective. As René speaks, the manager looks at his watch, makes no eye contact, turns, leans in, and whispers a few intimate words with Philip, who is sitting directly at the manager's right hand, then passes Philip a sheet of paper pointing to a specific paragraph. René continues to offer her suggestion, explaining the process for these town hall meetings. But other people in the room are now distracted as well. One woman is looking through her purse, someone else is flipping pages of a book—you get the idea.

Just as René is about to conclude, the manager cuts her off. And then with a smile the manager's right-hand man, Philip, chimes in, laughing almost facetiously, "Yeah, actually, town hall meetings are...you know, they're kind of 'been there, done that.' They're really not terribly effective."

While Philip is talking, we hear, through an audio voice-over, the thoughts of another participant, Javier. Javier is saying to himself, "René's got a really good idea there, but they never listen to her." Another comment or two is made about why town hall meetings really are not the best way to go. Then Javier says, "You know, I agree that Town Hall meetings are a little hokey (everyone nods), but what about introducing a series of open forums." At which point, the manager begins to look with a positive grin and gestures toward Javier, as though asking him to say more about how that might work.

Javier uses virtually the same words that René used earlier, but replaces "town hall meeting" with the words "open forum." The manager has a wide grin on his face and says, "I think you may be on to something there."

The other team members begin to nod in acknowledgment as well. The manager, looking for formal backing and reinforcement, turns to the team and asks what everyone thinks. Quite predictably, several other members offer their endorsement. There are no visible dissenters.

Throughout this part of the scenario, René slouches down in her seat, crosses her arms, and gives a very clear indication that her idea has just been stolen. Javier is then given a directive by the manager that he should pull this together and do whatever further research or focus groups may be needed to identify specific action steps to get this project moving. The manager offers, "When you have the outline and the proposal for this finished, I'll need to take it to senior team. Why don't you come along to that meeting with me?"

Javier, of course, has an ecstatic smile and is thrilled to be asked to come along to the meeting. Some other minor business is conducted and the manager adjourns the meeting. We hear René's thoughts in an audio voice-over: "That's the last time I bring an idea to this table."

All of us have probably been in René's position at some point in our career. You know the drill: You make a suggestion and it is met with a very bland, ho-hum response. Then, fifteen minutes later, someone else offers the same half-dozen as "six," and suddenly it shows profound insight.

Of course, sometimes the reason for this phenomenon has to do with the quality of our communication. Our delivery certainly influences how others hear what we say, but there are often other influences at play. Many times those influences have to do with who is doing the talking: Those old reliable filters step in and do their job quite well, and we do not see the gorilla in the room.

From the very beginning of the meeting, we instantly know that Philip and the manager have a close personal relationship. The three simple micromessages we saw made that entirely clear. We do not normally speak in a close intimate way with someone we do not know well, like, or feel close to. Second, we never make physical contact with someone we do not have a close relationship with. Third, we rarely laugh a sincere, hearty, genuine laugh with someone who is not a close friend or respected.

It becomes instantly clear why Philip is sitting at the immediate right hand of the manager. Being at the manager's right hand is far more than a literal seating position. Anyone watching that exchange could go into a meeting three or six months down the road. If they observe the manager and Philip walk into the room, they would never forget that the two have a close personal relationship, though they would probably not remember the micromessages that brought them to that understanding. Most people would forget that the manager and Philip touched, whispered, and laughed. But most everyone would understand that Philip and his boss are close buddies.

Now step away from the video scenario and think about what happens in real meetings in terms of the communication dynamics? Few people would dispute that it is the manager who determines how any meeting will play out. If you question that at all, merely think about what would happen if, while René was offering her suggestion, the manager had been looking directly at her, nodding, smiling, uh-huh-ing, and making other gestures that suggested he felt René's words were worthy of his attention. If the manager seemed interested in René's idea, would any of the others in that room have been looking through their bags, using their PDA, or doing anything else besides focusing their attention on René's remarks? Of course not.

Managers may not consciously think of it, but just as with René, when their attention is focused on what someone is offering, others in the room sense the manager's focus and start focusing for content and value.

It is immediately clear to everyone watching this scenario that while René is offering her suggestion, the manager is thinking to himself, "There she goes again, another one of her warm and fuzzy ideas. I do not need to pay that close attention. It's René. I've seen this all before."

Take a look at the following diagram. Which one of the two long vertical parallel lines is longer?

Did you say they were the same? Many people have seen optical illusion diagrams similar to this one before. But if you look a little closer, you will clearly see that the lines are *not* the same. They match at the top but definitely not on the bottom. The one that appears longer *is longer*. The one that looks shorter *is shorter*.

This is an example of the same phenomenon that drove René's manager to think those same words, "I've seen this before."

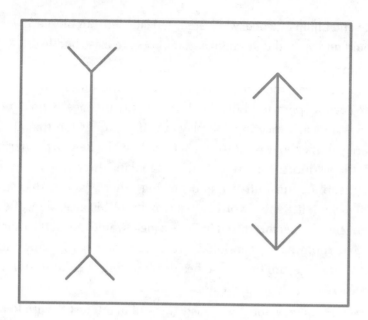

It is also precisely what we do with people throughout the work day. We look at someone and notice race, gender, age, height, style of dress, style of speaking—any number of dimensions—and we subconsciously say to ourselves, "I've seen this before."

Again, we subconsciously place them in a dull rat or bright rat category. Then the proverbial filters go into place. Of course, our "objective" conclusion ends up being remarkably similar to our assumption going in, influenced by, *I've seen this before*. We might genuinely believe we were objective, but a closer looks reveals we were utterly subjective: our unexamined prejudices dictated our point of view.

This habit of "I've seen this before" drives the ways we make decisions and view relationships of all types.

Do you remember René's final thought from the scene? "That's the last time I bring an idea to this table again."

It is certainly a very predictable response, and one that unquestionably will drive her participation (or lack thereof) and performance in future meetings.

One of your goals as an enlightened leader who understands micromessages is to make sure that you don't send microinequities that shut down the creativity and innovation of anyone on your team—your René equivalent.

CHAPTER 14

Bottoms Up!

I recently completed a presentation to a major corporation. During the question-and-answer segment, one of the senior managers put me on the spot. We were walking through ways to make the group's new awareness of the language of micromessages pay off in the workplace, and he said, "Frankly, I have no interest in *leveling* the playing field. The field is the field and it's up to the individual to make his or her own career." He seemed to have been holding back his opinion during the presentation and finally saw the opportunity to let it all out. "On the real field of play, athletes compete and the best person wins. We don't adjust anything and that's the way it works best."

For some reason, he thought we were on opposing sides and that effective micromessaging had something to do with coddling. But he was mistaken. In fact, having spent the better part of my life swimming with Wall Street sharks (no lawyer references here), I lived and breathed that logic every day. I had no interest in taking the piece of the pie I had worked hard for and cutting it up in order to share it with those who just limped along.

The manager seemed a bit surprised when I explained that we actually advocate taking his position one step further, not back. Since this meeting was being held in Las Vegas, I told him I would not only *see* him, but *raise* him a hundred. Here was my ante:

"Once you confirm someone is a substandard performer, don't waste another minute's time—jettison that person!"

Everyone we hire isn't going to make the grade. It's okay to want and expect the so-called best and brightest for your team, and since you are investing salary and resources for people to deliver results, you deserve the very best your dollars and environment can attract. He seemed taken aback, expecting a bit more opposition.

But this is where micromessages muddy the waters. How do you really know who your top performers are? To what degree are your checklist and filters giving you distorted data? If a manager is convinced that an employee is incompetent, how did he arrive at that conclusion? Whose lap did the employee spill coffee on? Or did she do something far less dramatic? Did she simply offend the manager by opposing him once too often? Or did the manager just not agree with her views on how to approach work? Did she get the same level of support, development, direction, and collaboration along the way as others did? Or did she actually become a poor performer because of the micromessages being sent by her manager?

Sometimes poor performers are easily identified, but other times you just don't know. How many times have we heard stories of people who are unceremoniously ushered out of the company because of their poor performance then become stars in the new company they join? Clearly the poor performance wasn't a lack of ability. There were other factors at play. When an employee is not meeting your expectations, you need to ask what role you might have played in getting them there.

> *Sometimes poor performers are easily identified, but other times you just don't know. They may clearly not be meeting your expectations, but what role might you have played in getting them there?*

Act on Your Short List

To evaluate your checklists and filters, start by ranking those who report to you in terms of performance, best to worst. Then compile a similar list of those with whom you work. Focus your efforts on the bottom one-third of both lists. These are the folks most likely to be receiving your most damaging microinequities. Write down the top two reasons they made either of your lists. You'll find yourself using expressions such as:

"They always..."

"Others on the team feel... "

"They don't have what it takes to..."

"Their sense of judgment is..."

You will probably find a shortage of the word "I" in your descriptions that define how and why they got to the bottom of your list. This could be an indicator of your level of involvement in their professional development process.

Next, jot down the word *hired* or *inherited* to define whether you personally hired that person onto the team or inherited him or her when you assumed the role. Place the numbers 1 through 3 by each name to indicate when you first came to your conclusion about the relationship: that is, (1) early/immediate, (2) many months into the relationship, or (3) after years of working together.

Finally, go back to the original assessment and incorporate a statement about your role once the perception was identified. It is likely that reading what follows may alter your perceptions. Here's what you are likely to see: A higher occurrence of "inherited" and "1s" (early/immediate). In the narrative about your role, look for a possible correlation between the inherited folks with 1s and the use of words such as, *told, reinforced, gave, showed*.

We are less likely to allow those we have personally interviewed and selected from a healthy list of often impressive candidates to slip into the lower performance ranks. When they do, it means one thing—we screwed up! Since we don't like to feel we screwed up,

We are less likely to allow those we have personally interviewed and selected from a healthy list of often impressive candidates to slip into the lower performance ranks.

instinctively, we send developmental micromessages which aid, encourage, assist, and inform. Oddly, you may not even see it as a problem, but rather a natural process of helping those we care about to succeed. In the aftermath of a merger it isn't uncommon to focus more on the well-being of those who come from "your" side of the merged teams. I have observed managers who actually revel in the failure of those from the opposite heritage company as a reinforcement of their own superior value.   Maybe we're a little like lions who defeat the alpha-male, then kill, or even eat, the cubs of the vanquished. Take care not to use someone's heritage as a factor in how you assess ability and provide support.

Do You Have a Level Playing Field?

Is it about loyalty? I observed the new CEO of a major Wall Street firm take the reins and dismiss every senior executive direct report in less than a year, replacing them with people he personally hired and had known for years. The decision had little to do with competency or skill and everything to do with trust. The upside of such a decision is that you know what you are getting and you're less likely to worry about your back. The downside is that you lose people who know the lay of the land, do the job well, and provide historical perspective and context. You can build loyalty. Don't let lack of it prevent you from holding onto the best talent.

I often think of a famous television beer ad from several years ago. The commercial begins and, out of the blue, someone looks into the camera and simply says, "Whassup?" That's it. Just those two simple words. I can only imagine sitting in the concept meeting when some brilliant team member said, "I've got it! The camera comes up on someone, they look directly into the camera, and say, Whassup!"

To be able to convince the company to invest an entire advertising campaign budget on a concept based on two meaningless words, that person had to have been perceived as one of the manager's top performers. If anyone else had proposed it, it would likely have been quickly panned.

Just imagine a less-favored employee offering that idea in the meeting; it probably would have been that person's last day on the job. Sometimes the decision assessing a person's worth is determined in your gut, and you just never recognize it. Objectively ask yourself, "How would I evaluate this work if my top person were to hand it to me?" It's often hard to clean that filter and see it through a new lens, but that is the only way you can objectively assess potential.

Forget that *level playing field* metaphor. Instead, think of providing every player with the same quality equipment and tools. No one on the team should get more practice time with the coach, or a higher quality racquet and, if some do, don't dump those who didn't from the team. That's not fair.

> *Forget that* level playing field *metaphor. Instead, think of providing every player with the same quality equipment and tools.*

Look at it in a social setting. Imagine you live in a neighborhood where, for the last several years, you regularly hosted dinner at your home for eight other couples. A new person (Carol) moves in next door. You invite Carol to join your monthly dinner party. When she arrives, you take her coat, welcome her, tell her if she needs anything just let you know, thank her for the house gift, then direct her to the appetizers. If you don't, don't at all be surprised if she ends up feeling left out and abandoned. It may be different in the workplace, but not so different for the less favored employees of the world.

You, the manager, ultimately set the tone for each employee's relationship with the company. Watch for the microadvantages you may have been sending your favorites for years. Put on a new filter. Assess the role those messages, and your relationship, have played in their performance. Confirm that poor performance isn't the result of your blind spot.

There are countless stories of people who left an organization where the chemistry was downright poisonous for them. Their poor performance history caused their termination to be recorded as "positive resignations." They went on to another company where they became a star.

Competitive profit-driven businesses cannot coddle lackluster employees, but leaders have the responsibility to accurately assess both roles in the performance equation—the manager's filters along with the employee's potential.

> *Confirm that poor performance isn't the result of your blind spot.*

It is hard to know what an individual needs to make their talent blossom. Analyzing the messages you send and receive can shine a brighter light on whether our conclusions regarding employee quality are based on fact or unexpressed emotions.

CHAPTER 15

Mixed Messages

Most international businesspeople know that when you exchange business cards in Japan, you are expected to offer the card with two hands and to receive it with two hands. A business card in Japan is an extension of the person offering it, so it cannot be casually pocketed, as is often done with business cards in many Western countries. Flipping someone's business card into your pocket in Japan would be similar to an American showing someone a photograph of his child, saying, "This is my daughter," and the recipient responding, "Great, thanks," and shoving it in their jacket pocket. What an insult!

Of course, we normally treat a photograph of someone—especially a family member—respectfully, as an extension of who they are. "My, what a lovely girl," we say. "How old is she? Where does she go to school?" We express personal interest.

In the case of the Japanese business card exchange, for example, the information on the card does more than tell recipients the other person's title and place of employment. Both parties are expected to look for what distinguishes each person from the other. It is a common practice to use the information on the card to determine where the other person stands in the hierarchy and hence how deeply each is supposed to bow to show respect.

As I read the card, if I learn your title is higher than mine, I know I must bow a little deeper. However, if the titles are equivalent, I need to find something else on that card to differentiate us. I look at your company to determine if you work for a more prestigious institution than mine. If they seem equal, I may have to go so far as considering office location, "Wow, you are in the Mitsuwa Building. Very impressive offices," I may say before I bow deeply.

Whatever can be found to distinguish levels of hierarchy determines the respect you get and receive. More immediately, it tells you how deep and how long and how many times you must bow.

Cultural Communication Styles

The anthropologist Edward T. Hall has written extensively about how the use of time and space can vary widely from culture to culture in the business setting.[1] He documents how South American meetings never begin on time. In that culture, the transaction of business could only take place after a long social chat—perhaps lasting hours on every conceivable topic except the business at hand.

He also describes how Americans, when given a large room in which to conduct business, will install themselves along the walls and leave the center of the space open to easily accommodate a new colleague. In comparison, the French, he says, claim space and give a new hire the smallest desk in the darkest corner.

Hall also describes how certain Middle-Eastern cultures feel the necessity to communicate very closely, so much so that they can feel one another's breath as they conduct business—a habit that makes most Americans and Europeans uncomfortable. He also explains that bargaining in business is a means of communicating and passing the time, as well as self-expression in Arab culture. Hall

---

[1] Hall, *The Silent Language*, 1959, 1990.

finds it wrong for Americans to project their pejorative word *haggling* onto a process that, to Middle-Eastern business people, is not only natural, but a necessary part of a business deal.

While conducting a multinational session in Europe, I asked people to describe their region's style of communicating and how they viewed the way other cultures' communicate. One woman, after describing how her culture communicates in a firm but respectful style, tending to take evenly spaced turns expressing thoughts, then added a perception about her Latin American counterparts. "When we talk to people in Latin America, they always seem angry or upset."

At that moment, a man seated at a distant table stood up, slapped his hand on the table, and said, "That's absolutely right! People always think we're angry." His eyes were big and his voice was loud. His hand kept slapping the table. "We're not angry. We're passionate!"

As the group discussed it further, we all understood and accepted he was right. I reminded those present, myself included, of this important factor: It is the cultural template of the sender that defines the accuracy of the message.

> *It is the cultural template of the sender that defines the accuracy of the message.*

If you want a good example of how people approach the business transaction internationally, observe how people stand on line in other countries. Many people in Mediterranean countries "cluster." when standing on line. Americans play by the (their) rules: they like fair, democratic, single-file lines. We'll allow someone's friend to join them, of course. And we will normally agree to hold the place of someone else. But try to jump line at a movie theater in New York City, no matter how well-dressed you are or whatever your skin color, and see what happens. Be prepared to take on the crowd.

Professor Hall tells of a Polish immigrant who told him he regularly crashed lines in the United States. Having suffered behind the Iron Curtain for too long, he told Hall that seeing Americans cue up like passive sheep in the face of authority drove him crazy.

Making Allowances

Of course, members of other cultures, like the Japanese, often give Americans and other foreigners the benefit of the doubt—even special dispensation—when they do not conform to explicit unspoken rules. We're stupid about the process, they believe, so they let us off the hook. This includes when we avoid using the nods and facial expression so common to them, which suggest power, dominance, and control.

An American is not, for example, expected to know the exacting rules for bowing in Japan: The junior person's bow begins at the waist and he folds to a near ninety-degree angle. There may even be slight multiple up and down motions. The hands are crossed at his waist or individually pressed to either thigh. When rising, the facial expression suggests deference and respect. Do it wrong and it becomes an insult.

In fact, the wrong bow between two Japanese businesspeople would simply not happen. It is as unlikely as a U.S. underling clapping the CEO, whom he's just been introduced to, on the back, while saying, "You're doing a great job, Bobby." Of course, conversely, if a CEO in whose corporation we are serving, singles us out, comes over, slaps us on the back, and says, "You're doing a hell of a job," we're honored.

One woman executive tells how she learned about bowing the hard way. When she arrived at her Tokyo hotel, the bellman carried her bags to the room, and she gave him a generous tip. The bellman bowed. She thought to herself, "Oh, you have to bow!" so she did.

The bellman then bowed again. She thought, "Oh, you have to do it twice." She bowed again. Then the bellman bowed once more. At this point, she confessed to the group she was thinking, "What the heck is going on here?"

She was sensitive about being thought of as the rude, "ugly American" so, she bowed again. You guessed it, the bellman bowed again. She said, "I felt as if we were caught in a loop and I didn't know how to get it to stop!" After about thirty seconds, she said to herself, "OK, enough is enough," and she stopped. The bellman bowed once more, waited to see that she wasn't going to bow again, walked backwards for a few steps, bowed once more slightly, turned, and walked off. She didn't learn until she returned to the States that the person considered on the lower level must bow last in this culture.

When there are simultaneous bows, it's never an issue since the senior person's shallow bow is completed long before the junior person is even halfway down. When the bows are sequential, the junior person has to be the last. In a first-class hotel, where one is paying for service over and above standard protocol, she was told that if she had continued bowing, the bellman would have kept going until the next morning.

As Americans, our cultural blind spots sometimes keep us from seeing the micromessages in other cultures. But careful and respectful observations can save us from projecting our own cultural bias when interpreting other cultures. The way of life of a people—their behavior patterns and attitudes—can be read through micromessages. By watching, we learn to understand things about a culture that go beyond spoken language. The result is better communication and greater effectiveness in business interactions.

> *The way of life of a people—their behavior patterns and attitudes—can be read through micromessages.*

CHAPTER 16

Micromessages:
In the Air and Everywhere

Have you ever pursued someone romantically, only to be rejected, without the word "no" ever being spoken? Maybe all you heard was how nice a guy you are, or comments of "neutral envy," such as, "Some girl is going to be incredibly lucky to have you someday." Letting someone down easy is a classic use of micromessaging that gets the message across, but leaves minimal collateral damage.

That message could be delivered face-to-face, over the phone, or even in voice mail and be just as effective. Micromessages are the central thread in every form of communication, including electronic communications. Our e-mails, voice mails, instant messages, phone conversations, and virtual meetings are all fully loaded.

A journalist friend, Sarah, told me that she could tell the degree to which her boss, an editor at a large city newspaper, liked the story she filed by the way the editor acknowledged the story in the e-mail reply. If the editor wrote, "Got it, thanks," as opposed to a simple, "Thanks," or even "Thanks, Sarah," it meant something different. The highest praise, Sarah knew, was when the editor bothered to use her name in the reply. "Thanks, Sarah"—that's

> *Micromessages are the central thread in every form of communication, including electronic communications.*

Be aware that your
inadvertent messages
may cause actions and
perceptions you may not
want.

when she knew she'd done a great job. A message like that always made her day. Her editor probably had no idea of Sarah's rating scale, but just as Sarah had hers, those who report to you probably have theirs. Your employees, consciously or otherwise, know how to size up your reaction to their work without your providing detail. At least they believe they can. Be aware that your inadvertent messages may cause actions and perceptions you may not want.

Investigate Assumptions First

Jay was the junior member of a team, and was eager to perform well. Over the weekend, he had been thinking about the team's project so Sunday afternoon, he sat down at his kitchen table and crafted what he felt was the perfect solution to one of the problems the team faced. He enthusiastically banged out an e-mail laying out his ideas and sent it off to the entire group, including the project head. Monday morning came and he waited for beaming faces to pop into his office and the pats on the back to begin. He checked the company's e-mail system, which told him that indeed everyone had opened his message from Sunday. But not a single person on his team, including Fred, with whom Jay was closest, responded. By noon, assuming everyone hated his idea, Jay pulled together his courage, walked into Fred's office and asked what his thoughts were.

Fred explained that he was waiting to hear from Margaret, the project leader, first. The culture of the team was to honor hierarchy. Margaret was the project leader so before anyone would offer an opinion, they waited to hear from her first. I am not assessing whether the practice was good or bad. The issue was that Jay was using his own filters to determine how others felt about his contribution. In their meetings, this was never an issue since the project manager was always present and could comment as an idea was being floated. Jay asked several questions about the practice and gained a robust understanding of the group's history and business practices that differed from his style. Had he not asked, he might have pulled back and been offended, putting a chill on his hot enthusiasm.

I have had managers who would only respond to a team member's e-mail when there was a problem or if a specific question was asked. In his case, silence was good news. It meant he liked what you sent and everything was fine. You only heard back if he was unhappy. If I looked at my new mail list and saw a reply from him, my heart would start pounding. It's amazing how the micromessage of a basic reply could cause such a strong emotional reaction.

Everyone has had the experience of receiving an e-mail that made you furious, only later to learn you completely misinterpreted the message. Jay took the right action in his case, practicing the most important lesson: Ask questions. Misunderstandings can be cleared up when you identify and clarify differences in business practices or communication styles. Sometimes it's better to leave your baggage behind and buy all new stuff when you arrive at the new location.

The story in *The Wizard of Oz* suggests the importance of investigating and pulling back the curtain to get to the heart of what underlies the ambiguous surface messages. Sometimes it's not a threatening figure, but an insecure, tired old man overcompensating for his perceived shortcomings. When the curtain is pulled back, you can turn your adversary into a supporter.

I routinely caution clients not to react too hastily to an e-mail message, because those same e-mails are often written in haste.

Translating thought to fingers and the time it takes to enter one character at a time is a process that encourages brevity. But sometimes brevity becomes cryptic and a message is distorted.

A few weeks after one of my seminars, Ellen called me and told me a funny but sad story about misreading a micromessage that came to her via e-mail, and how having her awareness raised in the session saved her a lot of grief.

Ellen had been working on a major presentation, but the day before it was to be delivered, she somehow deleted the file and couldn't recover it. Because this happened late in the afternoon and her presentation was the next day, Ellen enlisted the help of someone else in her area—a woman with whom Ellen didn't normally work. The colleague was agreeable and, in the end, helped Ellen to recreate the presentation in half the time.

Ellen was very appreciative. As she was leaving for the night, the woman mentioned having additional information at home that would be helpful for Ellen's presentation. She said she would e-mail it later that evening. Ellen was appreciative and said she would be on the lookout for it. As a point of reference, Ellen happens to be a very physically large woman.

That evening, Ellen opened her e-mail and found the data, which was indeed quite helpful. But at the end of the e-mail were the words: "You owe me big girl." Ellen said she was stunned. She thought she had been having a warm and collegial exchange with a colleague who might even become a friend. And from what Ellen knew of the woman, she didn't seem like the "mean girl" type. What to do?

The hurtful words were a real blow. As she told me the story she said that if she hadn't learned about microinequities, she would have either spent the day depressed, reported the woman, or just ignored it. But Ellen did none of these things. Instead, she filtered the experience through her new lens of micromessaging. She remembered how one sentence—"I did not say she stole the book"—could have six different meanings. So Ellen reread the offending sentence from the e-mail. She asked herself how she would punctuate what she read. In her mind, she had put a comma after the word, "me." To her the sentence read: "You owe me, big girl." She printed it out, went straight to the woman the next day and asked, "If

> *Be wary of misreading messages sent to you; clear up any confusion quickly.*

you were to put a comma in this sentence, where would it go? The woman read it and placed it after the word, "big." The intended message being, "You owe me big, girl."

"I always think about micromessaging now, and about what people are really saying to me, not what I expect them to say," Ellen told me.

Make an effort to send messages that empower—even when you are using electronic communication. Be wary of misreading messages sent to you; clear up any confusion quickly. And, of course, remember the power of nonjudgmental, neutral questions when making sure your messages are clear.

Micromessages Can Avert Disagreement

Part of the problem with electronic communications is that they take the place of our primary face-to-face method of communicating, and hence they deprive us of helpful micromessages. Electronic communications can take away the experience of a smile, a wink, a nod, the raised shoulders of exasperation, the defensive crossed arms, the narrowed eyes of judgment, or an alert eye-to-eye connection.

A pharmaceutical sales executive told me she has often observed how the company's elaborate electronic systems of communication simply are not an effective means for closing a deal. She is also a physician whose office is located in Europe. She told me that elec-

> *Part of the problem with electronic communications is that they take the place of our primary face-to-face method of communicating, and hence they deprive us of helpful micromessages.*

tronic meetings with colleagues—whether through e-mail, telephone conversations, or even teleconferencing with life-size screens between boardrooms—always seem to end with disagreement. All the technology and sophisticated gadgets in the world do not substitute for good old-fashioned human chemistry and being able to read the group's micromessages.

"Ironically, with all that technology, a lot more wires can be crossed," Dr. Gloria said, "When you are trying to reach an agreement via beamed light or sound, the dysfunctional people get more dysfunctional. The angry, disgruntled team players get more disgruntled. Misunderstandings grow rather than get resolved."

When this spirals out of control, Dr. Gloria usually convinces the higher-ups to fly all the players to one location. "There is something to be said for being in a room with colleagues. You can read them more clearly. It's almost hormonal, I think. We're all humans who want to reach an agreement and the small smiles we exchange, tilts of head, gestures of agreement, eyes that tell one another that each of us is taking the other side seriously, whatever it is, somehow help resolve the problems we might have been arguing over for months."

She said that the company has learned to bite the bullet and pay the travel costs needed for these face-to-face exchanges. Despite the expense of flying executives halfway around the world, the trips save money in the long run.

"Each day that we don't reach agreement and don't bring a product to market costs hundreds of times the travel expense," she said. "The company now fully supports putting us in one room where we are able to communicate with more than mere language."

As you learn more about how we send and interpret micromes-sages, you will see how we can use them to build stronger teams. Keep in mind that this process does not deplete the power of the leader or undercut office hierarchy. Rather, enlightened leaders can learn how *their* power can empower *others*.

CHAPTER 17

The Power of the Spell

Everyone in the room is watching my gestures like a hawk: what I do with my hands, my eyes, my entire body. They're also studying my tone of voice, my movements, my choice of words, my level of enthusiasm. What's going on?

We're playing "Catch Me If You Can," an exercise that helps bring any remaining nonbelievers fully on board with the power of micromessages and their influence on performance.

When the game begins, it appears I'm doing what we all do—I listen attentively to some but with a bit of distance to others. When someone answers a question I agree with, they get all the microadvantages you now know so well. When someone says something ambiguous or not in line with our prescribed approach, I find countless ways to make them want to shut down.

During the game, the audience's job is to sharpen their antennae and notice all I do. The first easily recognizable microinequity usually generates an immediate outburst. "That's a microinequity!" someone will shout.

At this point, attendees have grasped the message quite well, but they can still find it difficult to articulate what they see. When accused of turning my head while one person speaks, my natural, yet defensive, response is, "What's the big deal? I heard what she said. That's all that's important."

As someone speaks, I might do something as routine as merely staring into their eyes blankly. Certainly I have done nothing indictable, but the group feels the heat of my disapproval and the speaker shuts down in seconds. If I approached the speaker again, claiming to, "really want to hear what he has to say," I'm accused of lying. A follow-up to the group might be a firm, yet arrogant, "Listen carefully. I really want to hear what you have to say." I asked, "Who believes me?" Absolutely no one comes to my defense.

Around this time, I step out of the game and address the audience—partly to keep them from mass revolt. We talk about what happened in those few seconds. We analyze how I managed to make someone who might be a bright-shining star in someone else's eyes lose confidence, focus, vision—and, finally, the mental energy for the task before him. I remind my audience that this can happen to employees at *all* levels. In seconds, you can cause a confident, bright, aspiring individual to shut down and no longer participate—in an exercise, no less! If this happens in a scenario that everyone knows is "just a game," what does that mean for real workplaces and real-life situations?

In real time, of course, all of this is carried out a little more subtly. I caused the reaction in less than ten seconds. So if it's more subtle in the workplace, it may take ten times as long—100 seconds, or less than two minutes—to cause an employee to shut down. We could take it further. What if it took ten minutes—or even the entire space of a two-hour meeting? In all cases, it's clear that this chemistry turns toxic very quickly. Moreover, whether it's happening to you, or, conversely, you are the one putting it out there routinely, the message carries a big whammy.

The stark contrast between what participants are experiencing during the exercise versus the messages that were being sent over the past few hours causes a real sense of heat and antagonism toward me. Underlying the fun of the game, people quickly understand how my behavior has dramatically transformed participation. Even though people know this is only a game, there are those who truly lose respect for me. After hours of enjoyable interaction and enlightenment, I have become an offensive pig to several who were my biggest supporters just moments earlier.

When someone makes a particularly insightful remark, I might walk over, unclip my microphone and ask everyone to be quiet while the person restates his or her remarks. When they finish, a turn of the head and quick wink of approval causes an outburst of laughter.

One of the most powerful messages coming out of this game is that none of my behavior is aberrant. Everyone in the room acknowledges that practically everything I did has been seen in at least a few meetings within the past week. The people who receive microinequities babble and wither. Those receiving microadvantages give smooth, thorough, robust responses.

The impact on performance in that brief thirty minutes, driven entirely by subtle messages, is so evident that no holdouts remain. Even after the game concludes, the recipients of the microadvantages continue to actively participate while those having received the microinequities remain stuck in its aftereffect.

Still, describing how they know it is happening—what they *feel* in their bones—continues to prove difficult even for the most articulate of audiences. And let's face it—little of this could fall under "verifiable" discriminatory behavior.

Audience members are asked to identify which party in a meeting is the most powerful force for driving internal change; the sender, receiver or observer of the MicroInequity.. But as I continue to press the audience on who is really the most powerful force, they are forced to expand their thinking. Eventually someone comes up with the answer, "The observer!"

Some brief discussion makes it clear that the sender of the microinequity is just one person. The recipient of the microinequity is also only a single person. The observer of a microinequity, however, sits in a meeting and observes multiple interactions. If the person is an active observer, they can step in and intervene in numerous exchanges. The observer is also an objective third party. Being on the outside, the observer has virtually no baggage and will be listened to more openly, whether the observer's comments are made as the event occurs or in a private conversation after the fact.

Unanswered microinequities cause people to offer lower-quality responses and often shut down. Bestowing microadvantages encourages people to answer at length and with confidence.

> *Unanswered microinequities cause people to offer lower-quality responses and often shut down. Bestowing microadvantages encourages people to answer at length and with confidence.*

We never set this up in advance with the participants, but the results are surprisingly predictable every time. The "hands-on" experience further reinforces the power of these subtle messages and their impact on team performance.

As an active observer, I can intervene and go beyond having a positive effect on myself or someone sending me a message. I can have impact on the entire group, which is the most broad and powerful impact of them all. If we all serve as active observers, the force for transformation within the organization is incalculable.

In our "Catch Me If You Can!" exercise, we begin to raise awareness. But in real meetings every day, few are thinking about a connection between the messages the manager sends and the receivers' lack of participation. In the next chapter, you can experience this impact directly.

CHAPTER 18

Breaking the Spell

T he primary goal of effective use of micromessaging is performance improvement. The purpose is clear and communicated to all; nothing is clandestine or disguised. In fact, colleagues typically notice and appreciate the new messages being sent, and they are encouraged to reciprocate.

However, there is also a dark side to micromessaging. The process can be used to achieve our own objectives at the expense of others. Although most people gravitate to micromessaging because of what it has to offer in achieving business objectives, occasionally they make it "all about me."

> The primary goal of effective use of micromessaging is performance improvement.

The job interview is a classic environment for applying these skills in a self-serving way. You've probably had at least one job interview in your life where it was clear that the person conducting the interview had no intention of hiring you. It may be that the job was promised to someone internally, but Human Resources dictated that the job had to be posted for a certain number of weeks and a certain number of candidates had to be seen. Whatever the reason, you could have been Bill Gates, and it wouldn't have made a bit of difference. You weren't getting that job—you got the picture.

I've been in a few of those interviews in the course of my career. The person conducting the interview might as well have been looking at travel brochures, or take-out menus, because it was obvious they weren't thinking about my résumé. They give you the occasional nod and forced grin. Then, just as you finish describing a significant contribution at your current job, you look up for acknowledgment or a flicker of excitement and the only positive thing you get is a positively blank look.

If you're a little more self-confident than the rest of us, you may realize that the interviewer's failure to register interest in you isn't because you and your past work experience are boring or that the work was insignificant. Rather, they are just not listening. They are picking up a few catch phrases and sound bites here or there, but that's the best you are going to do today.

This is a microcosm of what happens every day in workplaces all over the world. Someone doesn't take us seriously or can't take the time to hear our point of view. And the result? We feel diminished. Sometimes the interpretation is quite clear. Other times even a micromessage master couldn't uncover what may really be going on in the interviewer's head.

How many times have you walked out of an interview believing you aced it, only to discover later you didn't even make the short list? You had terrific responses to the interviewer's question, you got wonderful feedback, you're a shoo-in, you think. Then, two days later, you get the dreaded letter dated the same day of your interview. The message is, "No, we don't want you, and we knew it the second you walked out the door."

Of course, most of us have experienced the reverse as well. You leave an interview sure you blew it. You come home and think: I really don't want to talk about it. That guy hated me the second I walked in the door. I babbled, was disorganized, and just blew it. A week later, you're asked back for a follow-up and soon after get the offer letter.

Frankly, you should never leave a job interview without knowing precisely where you stand, although getting the information can sometimes be difficult. The job interview is the one business meeting where people are specifically trained to be evasive about the messages sent, but the right questions can break the code. Reading the standard micromessages—smiles, nods, wows!—to assess your job interview performance can throw you off the mark. In interviews, the *questions* reveal the interviewer's true feelings.

This chapter looks at the dark side of micromessaging and how to break the spell. In almost every case, you will find that crafting the right questions is the most effective way to uncover what you really want to know.

Using open-ended questions or forced-list questions can get an interviewer to reveal more than may normally be given. However, this is not about asking your garden variety feedback question at the end of the interview. Each time you answer a key question, you should simply ask, "How would an approach like that work here?" or "Is that the sort of process that would be effective here?" These questions don't ask for the interviewer's assessment of you as a candidate. That's what they are trained not to divulge. They do, however, ask about the fit of a strategy with the company's culture. If the response is a "neutral positive," basically some version of, "Yes, that's fine," then you're probably not doing so well. In a normal business conversation such responses are positive indicators. Not so in the close-to-the-vest job interview.

> *In almost every case, you will find that crafting the right questions is the most effective way to uncover what you really want to know.*

Fortunately, asking the right questions of your interviewer may allow you to turn around a neutral interview well before you get up and leave. Don't allow the interview to end without asking this somewhat uncomfortable closing question: "I feel I've learned a lot about the position, the company, and your management style. I believe you've gotten a good sense of me, my skills, and what I could bring to the table. I feel there's a good fit." Now here's the climax. "If I weren't selected for this role, what might some of the reasons be?"

This is not the alternate close, common in the sales arena, which presents the respondent with a choice of two or three options. Instead, this open-ended approach requires elaboration. It also doesn't come out and ask directly for feedback about you and your candidacy. Instead, it asks for a list of items based on the hypothetical. Here's the range of interpretation:

- Most favorable response: "Actually, I can't think of any reason in particular..." That's it, you're in! Order the car.
- Recoverable response: "If you weren't selected the only reason might be..." Here's your chance for a comeback. Follow up with a response that answers the issues raised. Be careful not to start off sounding defensive. Consider an opening like, "I'm glad I asked that question. I might not have mentioned my work on..." There's no guarantee it will put you on the short list, but without posing the question, you would certainly have walked out not knowing how you stack up against other candidates. At least now you have a second chance at closing the deal.
- Game over response: "If you weren't selected for the position the reasons would be that..." If that sentence ends with three or more reasons, it just wasn't your day.

Role-Playing Exercise

The following exercise illustrates how quickly you can alter someone's ability to communicate. You can immediately feel the impact micromessaging can have on someone else's performance. It is best to try it with a colleague, but you can do it with a family member as well.

The exercise requires two people. First, decide which of you will be the speaker, and which will be the listener. The speaker, who is playing the role of the interviewee, speaks, and the listener, or interviewer, only listens. You'll find the hardest part of this exercise is keeping the listener quiet, because everyone wants to talk. You'll see why in a minute.

The speaker addresses each of the eight items in these two columns, starting with those in Segment 1 and then moving to Segment 2.

Segment 1	Segment 2
Name/tenure	Previous role
Position	Organization
Responsibilities	Responsibilities
Work challenge	Current project

For example, the speaker starts by giving his or her name, how long he or she has been with their current company, their current role, some key responsibilities, and a sentence or two about a current work challenge he or she is facing. The speaker does not stop. Go right on to Segment 2 and actually say the words *segment two* to let the listener know you have moved to the next column. Tell the listener about a previous role that you've held, the organization that it was with, some responsibilities you had in that job, then end with a sentence or two about a current project.

In Segment 1, while the speaker is speaking, the listener gives the speaker undivided attention. All eye contact, smiles, nods, and hums (uh-huhs, hmm-hmms) should make it clear to the speaker that there is nothing more important that what the speaker has to say. The listener finds what the speaker does absolutely fascinating. As the speaker completes the statement about his or her work challenge and moves to the next column, remember that the speaker should say the words *segment two* to alert the listener that he or she has moved to the description of past work experience, as listed in the second column.

As soon as the listener hears the words *segment two*, the listener should stop paying attention entirely. There should be no more eye contact from then on; the listener finds everything else more important than what the speaker is saying. He or she may search through a purse, check e-mail, or open a laptop. If you are the listener, you might look across the room for your friend and acknowledge your friend while the speaker speaks.

Be as clever and creative as you can about finding ways to show that you are distracted and not engaged in this one-way conversation. Feel free to make gestures with your head or hands, like you're impatient and the person should hurry up. Behave as if the sooner this person stops talking, the sooner we can all go home.

When the exercise is over, the first question to ask of the speaker is: What emotion did he or she feel on the receiving side of the Segment 2 behavior? Invariably, words like frustration, irritation, annoyance, anger, insignificant, and worthless are expressed.

The answers are particularly interesting given that people know that they were participating in an exercise—and they were told in advance what was going to happen. You can imagine how then, when these behaviors happen in the real world, the same emotions prevail, but are amplified.

What does this exercise tell us? We can find out by asking the speakers to describe their performance in both segments. People typically say in Segment 1, "I was a silver-tongued devil. I was delivering a message smoothly, thoroughly, accurately, and effortlessly." In Segment 2, I consistently hear comments like, "I lost my train of thought entirely. I was babbling and repeating myself. I found myself rushing through it. Segment 2 was significantly shorter than Segment 1. I could not remember simple things that would normally roll right off my tongue." It is not unusual to hear, "I lost interest in my own stuff." How do you lose interest in your own life? When you are sent microinequities, that's just what happens.

> *How do you lose interest in your own life? When you are sent microinequities, that's just what happens.*

This exercise is very powerful because it is an example of the hard-wired connection between micromessaging and bottom-line performance. In fact, the best way to understand this exercise is to do it, as suggested, with another person. Then you be the judge.

As the speaker, if you had to rate your performance on a scale of 1 to 5 (5 being the best) in Segment 1, when the person listening to you was attentive, how would you rate yourself? Nearly everyone who participates in this exercise rates their performance as a 4 or 5. How would you rate your performance in Segment 2, when the person listening to you was distracted and absent, and seemed as though he or she couldn't care less what you were saying? People consistently rate their performance as a 1 or 2. What does this tell us?

Micromessaging signficantly impacts performance. Segment 1 and Segment 2 were virtually identical; they covered the same basic topic (you), in front of the same audience, at the same time of day. The only thing that differed between Segment 1 and Segment 2 was how you were received, and how you were received did more than just affect your feelings; it affected your performance. You went from rating yourself a 4 or a 5 to a 1or a 2 in 60 seconds, driven entirely by how you were being treated. There should be no question, after this exercise, that there is a direct connection between how we treat people and how it causes them to perform. Micromessages can damage or enhance work performance.

Interestingly, I have noticed that senior executives tend to have a somewhat different reaction to this exercise than their employees—they tend to shut down more quickly when they get microinequities.

I was meeting with the executive team of a major auto company. We had a very limited time to present the material, and we were discussing ways to edit the seminar to fit into the allotted time. We decided to save some time by randomly picking someone from the audience for the Segment 1 and Segment 2 exercise and model it before the audience then debrief what was observed as a group.

> *Micromessages can damage or enhance work performance.*

So I randomly picked someone who ended up being the president of one of the major divisions. We began the exercise. During Segment 1, I was fully attentive and he was quite thorough and articulate in delivering the message. The moment he said the words *segment two*, I stopped paying attention, started going through my bag, grabbed a handful of potato chips, tossed them in the air and popped them in my mouth. I looked across the room, saw somebody I recognized, waved, mentioned his name and mouthed the words, "I'll talk to you when I'm done here."

At that point, I heard, in a very strong presidential voice, "Are you going to listen to me or what?" My response to him was, "I *am* listening. I can hear everything you say. Keep going." He continued, but at this point, I reached over, grabbed a banana, peeled it, started chewing on it, and turned my back almost entirely on him reading a distant poster on the wall, but used my hands to signal for him to keep going. "I'm listening to you, keep going."

At that point, he said in an even stronger tone, "If you don't knock this off, I am going to wallop you." What shocked me most was the word "wallop." I haven't heard that word since I was about ten years old, so I made fun of him. I repeated, with sarcasm "Wallop?" then said, "Go ahead, I'm listening, keep going."

He started once again, but this time we made physical contact. There was a bowl of grapes on a table behind him. I reached over, put my hand on the back of his shoulder, pushed him to the side and simply said, "Excuse me, I just want to get some grapes." At that point, he threw up his hands, turned and said, "That's it."

He walked straight to his seat, plopped down in his seat, crossed his arms, and looked in a different direction. For the moment, thinking less like a facilitator and more like a business owner, my first thought was, "Oops! Guess I won't be getting any more business from this company."

For the next three minutes, while debriefing the experience, he sat there slouched in his seat, sitting at an angle looking away, arms crossed, and moving his tongue around in his jaw. When responding to my questions, he would deliver a monosyllabic answer accompanied with the slow eye blink. (You have to do the slow eye blink in a mirror to get a sense of what that really tells you.) It took about three minutes, but at some point, he turned and started smiling, looked at me and said, "You know something? I was really angry with you! I hope you didn't think that was a big surprise."

He continued, "I forgot about this being an exercise, and I did what I would normally do if you and I were having this conversation and you did the things that you just did to me." He said, "I just realized something pretty important." He said, "I never get microinequities," and he looked at the other presidents of the major divisions in the room and said, "Neither do any of you. At our level, we don't get microinequities, but I am realizing that even someone with my skills and my focus can actually go from a 5 to a 1 performance rating in less than two minutes. And it had nothing to do with any of those things we normally associate with what affects employee performance."

He added, "I am sitting here thinking of the hundreds of thousands of people in this organization who may be getting messages, and how it must affect them the way it affected me. Even more importantly, they are probably just as unaware as I was of what is going on when they get these messages from their colleagues and their managers. All we need to do is have people understand this and, very likely, the change in those messages could have a huge impact on the performance of everyone who gets them."

Micromessages Can Be Used to Suggest Weakness

People can and will use micromessaging to control the environment and to keep ahead of the competition. Sometimes that competition is internal. Let's look at one instance of this more closely.

Following the announcement of a merger, a female executive, as the CEO of her company, and her male counterpart, the CEO of the other company, were named coheads of the corporation. A major meeting was held where both were to speak. The order was alphabetical, which placed her male counterpart first.

This very formal meeting commenced and, following some introductory remarks, the man was introduced and began walking to the podium. The audience was applauding, looking forward to hearing from both executives. After just a few steps, she stopped him, reached up to adjust his tie, then brushed the top of his shoulder, slapped him on the back, and sent him on his way.

He intuitively knew that something had happened, but nothing he could ever speak of. Should he thank her for straightening him up? Or condemn her for putting him down? Were her intentions honorable or something devious? From my vantage point, it seems one would need little more than the intuitive skills of a third grader to know that he had been relegated to being her little boy. I must have done those same sorts of maneuvers to my son a hundred times before sending him off to school. It seemed the one thing she left out after sending him on his way was a parental, "Now you be a good boy out there and make Mom proud."

It is unlikely the audience thought much of the exchange; they were too busy applauding. It was a microinequity that, in its silence, gave a clear impression of who was in charge. Incidentally, the decision was soon made regarding the leadership of the organization—she got the job!

Microinequities can be delivered as microadvantages, causing others to be put down. On the surface, offering help to someone in a way that implies an inability to get the assignment done well may seem supportive on the outside, but may have toxic effects. Your "kindness" can be damaging.

We can hide behind the mask of merely "asking a question," when, in fact, the question is a statement. Take the "question" mentioned earlier by my wife who often asks me just before stepping out for the evening. "Are you wearing that?" Does anyone really think that is a question? It is, by grammatical structure alone, but not by its intention. The obvious statement that comes ringing through is, "Take that ridiculous outfit off and change into something more appropriate."

Just as a question can be a statement, a statement can be a question. For example, if someone distributes resources in a way you feel is unfair, you don't have to ask a challenging question about their decision, rather, simply make a statement that serves as a question. "I couldn't help but notice that the resources were distributed in *this* way." The statement of your "observation" is a somewhat evasive yet nonthreatening inquiry about the person's decision. It will, of course, be read as a question.

There is a dark side to this skill. It can be used for sabotage and other illicit purposes, but this is the rare occurrence. Most people see the huge potential the skill offers to enhance our own performance and the performance of those with whom we work.

CHAPTER 19

Teachers at the Epicenter

"Adults are pretty useless when it comes to learning something new; that's why God created kids."—A seventh grader

By now you understand that micromessages are about more than trying to be fair or treating everyone equally. We are talking about a radical shift in perspective in every relationship that we have. We each need to become aware of the power of what we communicate—verbally and nonverbally.

Like the Wizard of Oz, we can choose either to embolden those who are uncertain of their potential or to play on their fears to frighten them back into unproductive patterns.

> *We each need to become aware of the power of what we communicate—verbally and nonverbally.*

Nowhere is the potential for change more clear than in the classroom. Here patterns are created that can profit future generations in many ways, including on the corporate bottom line.

Teachers are at the center of a metaphorical earthquake—something incredibly powerful. Although earthquakes have largely negative connotations, sometimes, even in the midst of destruction, unanticipated rewards emerge.

In San Francisco, for example, the elevated freeway system that blocked the waterfront was totally destroyed in the 1989 quake.

Rather than rebuild the freeway, the real estate industry and the city capitalized on new access to the waterfront constructing new buildings with incredible sweeping views of San Francisco Bay. Those views were not possible until the earthquake.

Like earthquakes, our educational system has teachers who are powerful catalysts and who spark the growth of young minds, although there are others who are purely destructive.

As the seventh grader quoted at the start of this chapter says, adults are sort of hopeless when it comes to real change. But if we can get teachers to recognize the power they hold in their hands, in the way they teach and relate to their students, they can be a powerful catalyst for change.

Schools are at the epicenter of cultural transformation. We want to shake things up in our schools so that the inequalities in our system and our cultural prejudices will not continue in future generations. Whatever we change at school will reverberate outward and have an impact on future generations.

As Dr. Robert Rosenthal's studies,[1] which we discussed in Chapter 10, showed, a teacher's expectations can create potential and achievement. When average students were treated like brilliant students, low and behold, by the end of the term they were performing like the "smart kids." When a teacher thinks, even without saying it, that Jose simply is not as smart as Craig it's likely Jose will get that message and live down to the teacher's expectations. Fast-forward to high school, Jose has had ten years of getting the message that he's not so bright. He instinctively will likely see high achievement as sour grapes and not desire them as a goal.

> Whatever we change at school will reverberate outward and have an impact on future generations.

---

[1] Robert Rosenthal, "Covert Communication in Classroom," 1998.

My own children have been so steeped in the subject of microinequities and microadvantages that they have become mini-experts on the subject. Over the years, they have come home from school with plenty of stories.

A Tale of Two Students

My son told me how he witnessed his teacher routinely treat two students in his class in drastically different ways: One of his close friends, Sam, would volunteer an answer, and the teacher would always respond with a flat, "No." My son put it this way: "Sam just can't get it right, even when he is. The teacher never expects him to get it right, and when he does, she simply says, 'Yes,' with no praise. Dori, on the other hand, is her pet. The teacher smiles at her when she raises her hand, and when Dori doesn't get it right, the teacher cuts her slack. She encourages Dori to try a little harder when her answer is partially correct. Eventually Dori gets the answer, of course, but if the teacher gave Sam the same treatment, he'd eventually get the answer, too. Sam just doesn't seem to care anymore."

Although Dori was only partially correct in her answer, the teacher's response was a warm engaging smile, a nod, and an outstretched arm, or so my son demonstrated. But, my son explained, Sam's answer was also partially correct. Even when the teacher called on Sam, she called on him differently: no smile, a floppy hand gesture that meant, "Okay you." But even if his answer was partially correct, the response was, "No, that's not it. Anyone else?"

Now, a thirteen-year-old does not know how to stand up to a forty-five-year-old teacher. An adolescent might find it a bit uncomfortable to tell a teacher, "That's a microinequity." But certainly, it's no surprise that when Sam receives microinequities for the balance of the class, he chooses not to say anything else. Why should he even try?

But, in this case, is Sam the only person negatively affected by the pattern of microinequities? No. The fact is that the teacher thinks Dori got the answer right, Dori thinks she got it right, and most of the kids in the class think she got the answer right. And everyone thinks that Sam got it wrong. When, in fact, both students were partially correct. Had Sam been egged on in the same way that Dori was, he might have gotten it "right" too. So a number of individuals were short-changed in this instance.

We are back to the filters: we see what we believe. It's a little like the 1983 movie, *Trading Places*, starring Dan Aykroyd and Eddie Murphy. Murphy's character had been a homeless person, and Aykroyd's character had been a spoiled-rich aristocrat. The joke, of course, is that as soon as Eddie Murphy takes over Dan Aykroyd's character's life—when Murphy is given the lavish life, unlimited support, professional development, mentoring, etc.—the world's filters see Murphy as a master of Wall Street; oh and so does Murphy. Aykroyd's character lives down to the hopelessness others expect from him. We quickly learn to play the role the world casts us in. If you're told you're seen as a street urchin, you begin to believe it, and that's what you become. It's the Pygmalion effect; a self-fulfilling prophecy.

> *We quickly learn to play the role the world casts us in.*

Another example of this, closer to home, was a little experiment we did with my daughter's friend, Trisha. She hated school and hated her teacher, so I suggested that she take her lunch during lunch period to the hated teacher's classroom, walk in and simply say, "I'd like to have lunch here today, please." She should wait for the teacher to speak. Once the teacher opened up the conversation, I told her she should ask the teacher questions like: "What made you want to be a teacher? If you were not a teacher, what other job would you be doing?" etc.

About four weeks later, when the student was visiting our home she said, "Mr. Young, you're not going to believe what happened. I did that lunch thing you told me to do and guess what I found out?" I could tell it was going to be good news. "I found out that my teacher has a twin. Guess who showed up for class?" she asked. She surprised me with, "The good twin. But guess who showed up for *class* later that day? The evil twin." She told me that she did the experiment twice and asked who I thought showed up for class *that* day. No surprise, the good twin.

The student has found a new love for learning. She has started to enjoy going to a class she had once hated; and she is excited to do the homework she had once loathed. Now she actually looks forward to interacting with a teacher whom she once despised. Not only that, the teacher has become her supporter and makes sure she continues to excel. The bottom line is: Trisha's overall attitude toward learning was transformed, and the teacher has no idea what caused the change. The student's microadvantages changed both of their lives for the better.

"This Is Good, for You"

My son offered me another real-life example of micromessaging in the classroom. But in this case, what looked like a microadvantage was a microinequity, and what looked like a microinequity was actually a microadvantage.

His teacher was handing back tests. As the teacher returned the test to the student on the left my son noticed he had gotten a score of 85%. The teacher said, "Terrific. Good job. " Then the teacher returned a test with the score of a 96% to the student next to him. This time the teacher's comment was, "What happened here? You should have gotten a perfect score on this. I'm disappointed in you."

Although seemingly negative, the real message implied the teacher thought very highly of the student and saw him as perfect. The other student's message was, "Holy cow, you got an 85%. I'm

shocked. That's really good *for you*." That pleasant-sounding con-
gratulation was certainly no microadvantage.

This was at the beginning of the school year, and the reason the
teacher may have made those assumptions was that the student
who did well had a long-term family history of high performers.
And the student who did poorly simply looked the part of the low-
income underachiever.

Unfortunately, many students who receive microinequities are
already stuck in a rut, while others are on the fast track. It becomes
more and more difficult to leap from the rut to the right track. The
fact is, we live up to or down to the expectations projected from
people with knowledge and authority.

> *The fact is, we live up to or
> down to the expectations
> projected from people with
> knowledge and authority.*

If you have children and you're
reading this on a school day, your
children are getting micromessages
this very moment. To the degree that
they learn how to read these mes-
sages and effect strategies for change in their classroom situation,
they can transform their own attitudes toward learning as well as
the ways they are viewed by their teachers.

In the classroom, children and teachers sit at the epicenter of
the potential for change in the achievement gap so prevalent in our
public schools. Becoming aware of the micromessages in our educational system may require the destruction of some old and comforting teaching habits. But as silent and coded prejudice falls by
the wayside, we can unlock the potential for every student to reach
his or her highest level of ability. Micromessages provide a critical
key to closing the achievement gap that educators have struggled
with for so long.

CHAPTER 20

Resetting Your Filters

So now you have the goods. You have the knowledge. Beyond the prescriptive elements laced throughout these chapters, how else can you use what you know to effect change?

Most of what you'll do with micromessaging will be more art than formula. Micromessaging is all about human dynamics; no absolute formula could ever work. Take what you feel makes sense and integrate those concepts into your routine business.

> *Micromessaging is all about human dynamics; no absolute formula could ever work.*

Mastery of the "art" of micromessages needs to incorporate the following three components.

1. **Awareness**, which strives to bring you to a state of knowledge and belief that the concept is real and powerful.
2. **Acceptance**, which implies buy-in. Once you not only believe micromessaging is legitimate, but believe in the concept as an advocate, then you can move to affecting change, becoming a catalyst by changing your own behavior and the behavior of others.
3. **Action**, which is the important step of taking your knowledge of micromessaging and converting it to have value. Don't hide this new information from others. Be

visible, vocal, and active about micromessaging to infuse the process into your corporate culture. Be an ambassador by getting others to collaborate with you.

People don't normally take action in support of a cause until they become convinced of its value. That requires passing through awareness and acceptance first. Some refer to these stages as head, heart, and hands; getting it, feeling it, and taking action.

Be aware that the many guidelines and tools presented within these pages, though effective for many, will not solve every problem relationship or make poor performers superstars.

The Levels of Learning

The first step of the action phase is to identify where you, and the relationship you will be addressing, are in the following levels of learning.

Level 1: Comprehension and Fluency

People at Level 1 have a fundamental knowledge of the concepts of micromessaging and an ability to see it when it happens around them. Level 1 people talk about micromessaging fluently, but are functionally oblivious to the microinequities they bestow. Disappointingly, many people never get beyond Level 1.

Level 2: Selective Application

Some who achieve Level 2 are fully aware of the micromessaging process. But they only take action when they are the personal recipients of microinequities. It's of interest to them only when it affects them, or they are hurt by it.

Level 3: Full-Time Awareness and Intervention

Those on Level 3 are fully aware of micromessaging and its impact. They are also very much attuned to how they send messages differently. Their choice of words, gestures, tone, nuance, and inflection is very much in line with achieving the performance they desire. They are also aware of when and how to intervene when they see microinequities being exchanged between others.

The Level 3 person goes well beyond awareness to recognize the three key roles played in this drama: the sender of the microinequity, the observer of the microinequity, and the recipient of the microinequity.

Understanding and Applying Learning

My most memorable example of a Level 1 manager was a person I encountered at a manufacturing facility in Montreal, Canada. In Montreal, the law requires presentations be delivered in both English and French. There is a time period within which to deliver the second language, but both must be provided. I had concluded one of my seminars that morning in English, and the plan was to have a meeting over lunch with a handful of employees to discuss the requirements for the French translation.

The head of the 5,000-person site was seated in the conference room with me and the folks chosen to discuss the translation. As we sat down, the senior executive leaned over and began explaining his extensive knowledge about social communications. He talked about Marshall McLuhan's communication models and various interpersonal communication theories. He seemed quite tuned into the impact of micromessaging on performance and relationships. "Wow," I thought to myself, "This guy will be great at modeling the process top down to the organization."

But no more than five minutes into the meeting, someone commented about a possible time conflict with our translation and rollout of the microinequities program in six months, and the release of one of the company's new products, which was scheduled for release in five months. The senior executive leaned forward, furrowed his brow, extending his hand across the table, pointed his finger at the person who had made the remark, and said, "Five months? It's not five months. You don't know what you're talking about."

He may have done extensive reading about communication theory and its impact on employees, but he probably should have focused more on comprehension. The behavior of those in the meeting fell predictably into place. Not surprisingly, the person who received the tougue lashing remained silent through the balance of the meeting, only nodding occasionally to show attentiveness.

This case aside, it's encouraging that so many corporate executives do latch onto the concept of micromessaging so quickly. They zero-in on the association with performance and walk out eager to test its influence on their staff.

On the other hand, some intellectuals and academics seem a bit slower to grab the ring. In some cases, their behavior can be a veritable wrecking ball. In my many years of doing this work, it has become clear to me that intelligence is no measure of one's ability to master this skill. In many cases, there is an almost inverse correlation between intelligence and obliviousness to microinequity behavior. Start with the apex of academic icons and hover in their stratosphere to observe an abundance of micromessage faux pas.

At the most prestigious academic institution in the United States, the president recently made an inadvertent quip about women and their lack of natural ability in the sciences. It would prove to be his undoing. A few words wrongly placed got him *displaced*. Intellectuals of his stature often have a propensity for resisting change in behavior when it is, they believe, the behavior that in part got them to the heights they have achieved.

Ironically, the hybrid—the academic who teaches business— seems to get it at light speed, as I observed with staff members at the Harvard Business School. Very possibly, educators and academics may subconsciously feel the enormous burden resting on their shoulders, knowing that micromessaging is at the core of how students learn. How well educators micromessage shapes how students open up to learning, their accomplishments and self-esteem, and the direction of careers.

How well educators micromessage shapes how students open up to learning, their accomplishments and self-esteem, and the direction of careers.

There are many others in authority who, even after being informed, remain resistant to change, and in their attempt to repair the damage, only exacerbate the problem. When U.S. Senator Trent Lott spoke at an event honoring his long-term congressional colleague Strom Thurmond, he made the following remark:

"I want to say this about my state: When Strom Thurmond ran for president, we voted for him. We're proud of it. And if the rest of the country had followed our lead, we wouldn't have had all these problems over all these years, either."

Thurmond ran as the presidential nominee of the breakaway Dixiecrat Party in the 1948 presidential race. He carried four states and, during the campaign, said, "All the laws of Washington and all the bayonets of the Army cannot force the Negro into our homes, our schools, our churches. We stand for the segregation of the races and the racial integrity of each race."

Lott may have believed, more than a half century after Thurmond's run, that he was just offering an idle hyperbole of kind and supportive remarks for an old friend at his 100th birthday party. He couldn't have been more wrong.

Lott's remarks gripped the country like a political python, nearly squeezing the life out of his illustrious career. The micromessage seemed to lament not having a country run like the good old South.

Lott's biggest mistake, however, and the biggest mistake people commit when they find themselves mired in a microinequity mudpool, was not the remark itself, but the defensive response. His first remarks were to tell those who reported and analyzed his statement that they had misinterpreted him and were wrong. That sort of defensive response is deadly.

When Lott felt the constricting squeeze of public opinion continue to tighten around the life of his career, he decided to apologize. He said, "A poor choice of words conveyed to some the impression that I embraced the discarded policies of the past. Nothing could be further from the truth, and I apologize to anyone who was offended by my statement." The micromessage laced through the apology reinforced the reason one was needed in the first place.

The apology conveyed an act of compliance, not contrition. It wasn't an apology, it was protective spin. I'm sure he felt he had genuinely apologized, but the micromessages laced throughout revealed it had been stated under duress.

It took several days, but a new apology was crafted that said all the right things and was a model of micromessage mastery. "I apologize for opening old wounds and hurting many Americans who feel so deeply in this area." He asked people to "find it in their heart" to forgive him, and vowed to work with community leaders to make amends. "Segregation is a stain on our nation's soul and represents one of the lowest moments in our nation's history. I will dedicate myself to undo the hurt I have caused," Lott said.

This micromessage conveyed remorse, disappointment, clarification, and a commitment to change behavior. It is wonderful when

our hearts and our heads are in concert. When they are of different beliefs
we must yield to the head particularly
in our responsibilities as leaders. Lott's
second apology reflected the actions of
a wise, team-focused leader.

> *You don't need to be disingenuous in an inappropriate way in order to effectively use micromessages.*

Let me reinforce that none of the
concepts or practices in the mastery of micromessage management
requires you to be anything less than genuine about your true feelings and values. You don't need to be disingenuous in an inappropriate way in order to effectively use micromessages.

Teachers who use micromessaging effectively provide balanced
attention and interaction with every child in the class, regardless of
how he or she may feel about the stu-
dent personally. The teacher's job is to
fill students' minds with knowledge,
build self-esteem, and encourage
them to live up to their potential. The
job of the leader is much the same,
but the leader also needs commitment and loyalty in order to develop
a team that will outpace others.

> *The teacher's job is to fill students' minds with knowledge, build self-esteem, and encourage them to live up to their potential.*

What Micromessaging Is and Isn't

Look for opportunities to call the Emperor's see-through suit what
it really is as well as explain the concept of micromessages thoroughly to others. You might encouter some attempt to use the concept of multitasking to neutralize microinequities. You'll then have
the opportunity to set them straight.

Many people herald multitasking as an admired and needed
skill—something that demonstrates one's commitment to produc-

tivity maximization. The concept is relatively new—only a couple of decades old. Normally, when new concepts appear on the business landscape, there is a desire to demonstrate your knowledge and skill with the new concept to those who evaluate your performance—your boss and the leadership team. Strange though, how that practice doesn't hold true for multitasking. It's not a common practice to tell your manager, when she strolls into your office, "I have to keep writing this e-mail. Keep talking, I'm listening." Go ahead, just try it!

The concept originally addressed the need to juggle multiple projects. Recent workload increases and expanded breadth of control require workers to manage multiple core projects with different directions, deadlines, and participants. There is a need to be able to spin around, turn on a dime, and respond to the demands of any of those tasks. The concept of multitasking signaled that the days of being able to remain focused on one single project to its completion were gone.

The concept was not, however, about simultaneous brain functioning. No one is really expected to type an e-mail with the left hand, sign requisition authorizations with the right, listen to a conference call on a headset, while reading a document from aclient. Don't call that multitasking—call that madness!

> When your engagement is required, giving your focused attention is a strong microadvantage that enhances your performance, as well as the ability of all those you might otherwise disengage from.

Yes, you can read that occasional e-mail when you've been put on hold, or when the activity around you doesn't require your engagement. When your engagement is required, giving your focused attention is a strong microadvantage that enhances your performance, as well as the ability of all those you might otherwise disengage from. The term *multitasking* has merely become an excuse for not having to pay attention when you don't want to, which is just another microinequity.

As you go about observing micromessages and being an advocate for change, be careful not to confuse cultural differences as microinequities. Bowing, lack of eye contact, enthusiastic hugs of greeting, cold demeanor, and passionate expressions convey different messages based on one's cultural filters.

Choose Your Seat Wisely

A microinequity is usually just a symptom of some other issue. Much of the focus in the action phase is about resetting filters to uncover the message behind a symptom.

We must look more deeply to locate and understand its source. Sometimes the inaudible messages observed by just walking into a room can reveal a great deal about relationships and hierarchy. Step into an auditorium or large function room for a department or large group meeting. Scan the room as the meeting gets under way. You will be able to identify the social hierarchy by where people choose to sit. At any large meeting, the front few rows tend to be where the most senior attendees sit. Although not precise for every business, the self-selected seating segments go front to back by rank.

The subsequent set of rows tend to be occupied by those next in rank, people with high tenure and the "anointed ones" identified as the emerging top talent. As with the ocean, this wave lays down different groupings of pebbles and sand all the way up to the shoreline. The people who go for the seats in the back of the room may not be aware of the message they are sending. The rear seats tend to be chosen by those whom fear being singled out, are low in hierarchy or influence, or may just need to discretely leave early that day. What message do you want to send? Sitting in the rear communicates a silent, but clarion, bell of where you feel you fit into the hierarchy. Choose your seat wisely. Unconscious silence can speak for you.

Where you sit, how you greet, where you look, whom you ask, how you apologize, when you interrupt, how you challenge, and how you do nothing at all tell a story. They also tell others their roles in the story, particularly, who gets the leads, the supporting roles, the understudy role, who is in the tech crew, or who becomes the usher. Once the show begins, it's usually quite difficult to change roles.

Look for micromessages that reveal interest and talent and open those windows when you can find them for a fresh breeze of opportunity.

Audition the talents of your team frequently and, most importantly, throw out your old filters. Look for micromessages that reveal interest and talent and open those windows when you can find them for a fresh breeze of opportunity.

The following microadvantages top-ten list can be a pivotal catalyst for turning around problem relationships. Use these ten steps to improve your use of micromessages for a positive impact:

1. Actively solicit opinions
2. Connect on a personal level
3. Constantly ask questions
4. Attribute/credit ideas
5. Monitor your facial expressions
6. Actively listen to all
7. Draw in participation
8. Monitor personal greetings
9. Respond constructively to disagreements
10. Limit interruptions

All ten microadvantages can be applied to any relationship without violating your values or misrepresenting your opinions of others. You will, however, fertilize and unlock participation, creativity, and innovation.

The power to drive change is with the ants, not the elephants. The power of the small has always held the force to alter our lives. Our attention tends to be drawn by the big and the obvious, but whether it is the tiny seed that is the basis for all life, or the microscopic bacteria and viruses holding the power for all

> *The power of the small has always held the force to alter our lives.*

life's destruction, what you don't see can either kill you or support you. The smallest micromessages can either kill relationships or your career or, if managed well, make it stellar.

Harness the micromessages that are the seeds of great leadership. Your continued subtle pruning will bring them to their greatest heights and yield the best possible fruit for your nourishment, advancement, and enjoyment.

Afterword

J ust as I was finishing writing this book, I presented my program
to a company in northern California. Afterward, the senior manager, Eduardo Salaz, who had coordinated the seminar for Intuit,
presented me with a Talking Stick. The Talking Stick is a carved
piece of wood that is decorated, often with feathers, beads, and

leather. It is a sacred object that has been part of indigenous cultural tradition for centuries.

The Talking Stick is a tool to facilitate conversations for deep understanding and respect. It is passed within a group—any group, a family, even competing tribes. The holder of the stick has the "word" and is responsible to speak the truth in a way that respects self and others. Everyone else in the circle must listen carefully. There's no place for attention deficit disorder when the Talking Stick is present.

When the Talking Stick is passed to an individual, it emboldens its bearer to speak the truth from a deep place. But the Talking Stick demands that everyone else present hear the full message being delivered. No one else may speak, or leave the circle, or otherwise break the concentration of the group on the person using the Talking Stick. The holders do not feel the need to monopolize the group because they realize they are truly being heard.

It occurred to me that the art of reading micromessages is similar to the ritual of the Talking Stick. Reading micromessages requires the time and presence of mind to listen more than on the surface to what someone is saying. In turn, this opens new channels of communication in much the same way as Native Americans have used the Talking Stick as a conduit for communicating and connecting with others.

Many of the concepts advocated here are relatively easy to implement. In fact, sometimes some of the most effective solutions are rooted in the most basic concepts. I often think of the early days of medical surgery. There was a time when surgeons first learned how to cut open the human body, remove organs, repair them, return the organs to the body cavity, close the wound, and the patient was healed. This was a truly remarkable accomplishment. But what was the greatest cause of postsurgical death? Infection!

The skill was there, but the lack of awareness of the importance of sterile conditions allowed for the introduction of bacteria. There was the apparent belief that if something was washed and visibly clean, then it was clean. This is the ultimate example of *what you don't see can kill you.*

Micromessages are similar in many ways. You don't typically see them, yet they can kill your career or a relationship. Tuning into their frequency can enable you to see what has been invisible, discuss what is never talked about, and catapult normalcy into excellence.

Index

About the Author

For more than a decade, organizational guru Stephen Young has brought his powerful message about micromessaging and leadership to executives in businesses spanning fifteen countries. In 2002 Young founded Insight Education Systems, a management consulting firm specializing in leadership and organizational development, applying these concepts to nearly 10 percent of the Fortune 500 and to many of their CEOs and leadership teams. Previously, as Senior Vice President at JP MorganChase, he managed the firm's worldwide diversity strategy. Under his leadership, the company garnered numerous awards, including the Catalyst Award and a place on *Fortune Magazine*'s list of Top 50 Companies for Minorities, and it was ranked the number one company for diversity by *Inc* magazine.